Vol. 1

Contents

Nana - Nana Komatsu 3
Nana - Nana Osaki 105
Junko 177

SURROUNDED
BY MOUNTAINS...

MY HOME TOWN
IS NEITHER
BIG NOR LITTLE.

IT ISN'T A BIG CITY OR A
TINY VILLAGE WAY OUT IN THE COUNTRY.

THERE WAS NOTHING THAT REALLY SOLD
THE TOWN FOR TOURISM.

I WAS THE MIDDLE OF THREE DAUGHTERS.

LEFT TO MY OWN DEVICES...
BY PARENTS WHO WERE NEITHER
RICH NOR POOR...
I GREW UP QUICKLY.

I WAS JUST ABOUT TO
GRADUATE FROM...

AN AVERAGE, LOCAL,
ALL-GIRL HIGH SCHOOL...

NANA

ナナ

TOKYO?

UH-HUH.
FFTT
STARTING NEXT WEEK.

HANG ON A SEC...
YOU MEAN THIS ISN'T A BUSINESS TRIP, BUT A...?
BRRUMM
...A TRANSFER.
I...
I HATE THIS!!
THE MAIN OFFICE IN TOKYO JUST TRANSFERRED ME ALL OF A SUDDEN.
WHAT A PAIN.
WELL, I HAVE TO SAY IT'S A WELCOME CHANGE IN THIS ERA OF CORPORATE RESTRUCTURING.
BUT WAIT!
TOKYO'S ONLY TWO HOURS AWAY BY BULLET TRAIN.
drip drip
IF I WANTED TO, I COULD EASILY SEE HIM.
THIS ISN'T THE MIDDLE AGES...
BESIDES, WE DON'T SEE EACH OTHER VERY OFTEN ANYWAY, SO...
IT'S GOING TO BE LONELY...
NOT BEING ABLE TO SEE YOU ANYMORE, NANA.
BUT IT'S WORK, SO WHAT CAN I DO...?
IT'S ALL BEEN GREAT, HANGING OUT WITH YOU.
VROOM
THANK YOU.

THAT WAS IN MARCH OF 1999 ...
... FOUR MONTHS BEFORE JULY.
HOTEL Tiffany
OUT
THE DEMON LORD OF TERROR SOUGHT ME OUT AND CAME CRASHING DOWN.

I ALREADY KNEW ...

THAT THIS RELATIONSHIP DIDN'T HAVE A FUTURE.

BUT TO END SO SUDDENLY?

SO CARELESSLY?

IT WAS POINT-LESS TO SHED ANY TEARS.

YOU'RE CRYING THOUGH.
BUT...
Uhh... Uhh...
Waaa...
JUNNNN?!
THAT'S WHY I TOLD YOU TO CUT IT OFF.
A MERE HIGH SCHOOL GIRL INVOLVED IN A CHEATING RELATIONSHIP...
DON'T SAY "CHEATING"!!
IT MAKES IT SOUND LIKE A COUNTRY SONG!
THEN WHAT ABOUT "PROSTITUTION"?
JUN!
I HAVEN'T RECEIVED A SINGLE CENT FROM TAKASHI!
AND YOU KNOW THAT!
YOU'RE SUCH AN IDIOT...
YOU SHOULD HAVE GOTTEN WHAT YOU COULD OUT OF HIM...
'CAUSE HE GOT A FREE RIDE.
JUU...
WHADYA MEAN A FREE RIDE...?
BUT IF YOU LOOK AT IT FROM HIS SIDE, IT WAS ALL JUST A GAME, I GUESS.
STAB
HE PROBABLY JUST THOUGHT YOU'RE A TEENYBOPPER THAT JUST BLOSSOMED....
I'M KIDDING, NANA.
I KNOW YOU WERE SERIOUS ABOUT THIS GUY.
JUUUUNN...

TEENY-BOPPER?!
WHAT PART OF ME IS...
AND WHADYA MEAN "BLOSSOMED" ...??!
IN THE EYES OF OLD MEN, ALL HIGH SCHOOL GIRLS ARE TEENY-BOPPERS.
TAKASHI ISN'T AN OLD MAN!
HE'S ONLY IN HIS 20s!
COMPARED TO A HIGH SCHOOL GIRL, ALL "SUITS" ARE OLD MEN.
WAS I STUPID FOR GETTING A HAIRDO LIKE NORIKA FUJIWARA?
WHAT ARE YOU TALKING ABOUT?
I MEAN, IS THAT SUPPOSED TO BE A NORIKA HAIRDO?
SO THAT'S WHY HE THOUGHT I WAS A TEENY-BOPPER...
BUT HE'S AN ADULT, SO I THOUGHT I SHOULD TRY TO MAKE MYSELF LOOK A LITTLE MORE MATURE.
I TRIED SO HARD, SPORTING HOT OUTFITS ON OUR DATES!
UH-OH.
THAT'S PROBABLY WHERE YOU WENT WRONG...
YOU TRIED TOO HARD.
WHY IS IT THAT NO MATTER WHAT I DO, NOTHING EVER WORKS OUT?
BESIDES, THE NAME "NANA" IS BAD LUCK.
I COME UP IN NOSTRADAMUS'S PROPHECIES...
MY NAME'S IN SCARY MOVIES...
LUCKY SEVEN, WHAT A LIE!
I'M JUST CURSED...
NO...
I THINK HE WOULD HAVE GONE TO TOKYO ANYWAY.
BUT TOKYO...
HE'S SO LUCKY.
YOU KNOW, I SHOULD'VE APPLIED TO A TOKYO ART SCHOOL, TOO.
NO WAY!
I'D DIE IF YOU WENT TO TOKYO TOO, JUN!

BUT I UNDERSTAND.
OF COURSE YOU'D LOVE TOKYO. ♡
THERE'S A LOT OF COOL SHOPS...
AND YOU CAN GET YOUR HAIR DONE AT THE BEST SALONS.♡
I SUPPOSE.
THAT REMINDS ME, A CUTE SALON JUST OPENED UP NEAR THE F TRAIN STATION, MAYBE I SHOULD GO.
I WANNA GET A PERM.
SO OKAY!
LET'S GO!
HUH? YOU'RE CUTTING IT? YOUR HAIR?
WHILE YOU HAVE A BROKEN HEART?
IT'S ABOUT LOOKING FORWARD TO MY NEXT RELATIONSHIP.
I'M GONNA GET A HAIRDO THAT WON'T MAKE ME LOOK LIKE A TEENYBOPPER ANYMORE!
Na-na- ♫
Na na-
Na-na-na-
BUT AFTER TODAY, YOU'LL BE A HIGH SCHOOL GRADUATE.
YOU WON'T BE A TEENYBOPPER ANYMORE, YA KNOW?
NO WAY!
THE GRADUATION CEREMONY'S ALREADY STARTED!
OH NO!

LOOKING BACK, MY HIGH SCHOOL LIFE...
STARTED AND ENDED WITH LOVE.
AND THAT'S NOT AN EXAGGERATION.

IT WAS IN THE SPRINGTIME OF MY FRESHMAN YEAR...
DISAPPOINTED AFTER STARTING AT AN ALL-GIRL HIGH SCHOOL WITH NO CHANCE OF EVEN MEETING ANY GUYS...

I INSTANTLY FELL IN LOVE WITH MR. OKAMOTO, MY 25-YEAR-OLD TEACHER FROM ART CLASS.

I WASN'T PARTICULARLY GOOD AT ART...
BUT I DECIDED TO JOIN ART CLUB WITH THIS GIRL FROM MY CLASS, JUN, WHO I SOON BECAME FRIENDS WITH.
I WAS ALWAYS GOOD AT ART.
YOU'RE QUITE GOOD AT DRAWING.
TEE HEE ♥
AT ANY RATE, THAT'S HOW I GOT INTERESTED IN DRAWING.

I SHOULD HAVE PROFESSED MY LOVE TO HIM.
IF YOU DON'T SAY ANYTHING, NOTHING WILL EVER HAPPEN.
NEXT TIME I WILL, I SWEAR!
I SUPPOSE... BUT THERE'S ALWAYS A CHANCE YOU'D MAKE A MOVE, AND STILL NOTHING WOULD HAPPEN.

BUT AFTER THAT YEAR, NOTHING REALLY HAPPENED BETWEEN US, AND THEN HE TRANSFERRED TO ANOTHER HIGH SCHOOL.

MR. OKAMOTO ...
I WAS GROWING OUT MY BANGS SO I COULD HAVE THE SAME HAIR AS YOU...

MY NEXT ROMANTIC ENCOUNTER CAME SOON ENOUGH.
HOW MANY DAYS WILL YOU BE RENTING FOR?
中村
MEET MR. NAKAMURA, AROUND 23 YEARS OLD, THE HIPSTER WHO WORKED AT THE VIDEO STORE NEAR MY HOUSE.
UNTIL TOMORROW. ♡
I WENT TO THE VIDEO STORE EVERY DAY, JUST SO I COULD SEE HIM.
TRYING TO IMITATE HIS HAIRDO.
青春ラブロマンス
SO THAT'S HOW I GOT REALLY INTO MOVIES.
BUT THEN ONE DAY, WHEN I FINALLY GOT THE GUTS TO TALK TO HIM, HE BLEW ME OFF.
UM...
LET'S GO OUT!
UH...
THAT'S KINDA INAPPROPRIATE.
貸出カウンター
HAVE A NICE DAY.
I PROBABLY SHOULDN'T HAVE BEEN SO FORWARD.
NEXT TIME, I'LL BE LESS OBVIOUS.
NOPE.
EVEN WHEN YOU PLAY IT COOL, BAD IS STILL BAD.
AND THERE WERE FUTURE ENCOUNTERS...
LIKE THE OH-SO-COOL MR. KAWASAKI, 35 YEARS OLD. HE'S THE CHEF AT A RESTAURANT I WORK AT PART TIME.
BUT FOR SOME REASON, NOTHING EVER CAME OF MY ROMANTIC EFFORTS.
THANK YOU
吉田
THEN THERE WAS THE BABY-FACED PIZZA DELIVERY GUY, YOSHIDA, PROBABLY AROUND 20 YEARS OLD.
IT'S PROBABLY BECAUSE I WASN'T CHARMING ENOUGH.
SO I DECIDED TO GO ON A DIET.
YOU SURE THAT'S THE PROBLEM?
THESE DIET COOKIES AREN'T SO GOOD.
BUT, WHY DO YOU ALWAYS FALL SO EASILY IN LOVE LIKE THAT ANYWAY?
MEN ARE ABOUT WHAT'S INSIDE, NOT JUST HOW THEY LOOK, YA KNOW?

IT'S TRUE, I WAS MORE CONCERNED ABOUT LOOKS THAN MOST PEOPLE ARE.
BUT NO MATTER HOW HOT A GUY IS, I WOULDN'T LIKE HIM IF HE WAS EMPTY INSIDE.
SO THEN WHY ARE ALL THE GUYS IN THE MOVIES SO GREAT?
I WONDER IF THERE ARE ANY GUYS OUT THERE SOMEWHERE WHO ARE THAT COOL AND NICE IN REAL LIFE ...
Stagger
Stagger
WHAT THE ...?
I FEEL LIKE I'M GONNA FAINT.
Stagger
I REALIZED THAT I REALLY HAVE TO START TAKING THE TIME TO GET TO KNOW THE PERSON BEFORE I FALL IN LOVE AGAIN.
BUT THIS WAS JUST A FLEETING THOUGHT.
IT WAS THE BEGINNING OF THE SUMMER OF MY JUNIOR YEAR IN HIGH SCHOOL...
WHEN I FINALLY MET HIM.
HEY--
WHAT HAPPENED-- ARE YOU OKAY?

OH.
I'M SORRY...
YEAH, I'M OKAY.
YOU'RE TOTALLY PALE.
YOU SHOULD LIE DOWN FOR A SECOND ON THE BENCH HERE.
NO...
I'M OKAY, REALLY...
YOU SHOULDN'T OVERDO IT.
I'LL GO GET YOU SOMETHING TO DRINK.
ENTER TAKASHI ASANO, AGE 29.
NOW THAT I THINK OF IT, HE MIGHT HAVE USED A PSEUDONYM.
HE MIGHT HAVE LIED ABOUT HIS AGE, TOO.
IT WAS LOVE AT FIRST SIGHT.
HAVE YOU EATEN ANYTHING?
NO...
I'M ON A DIET, SO SOMETIMES I GET DIZZY...
YOU'RE SO CUTE JUST THE WAY YOU ARE, WITHOUT HAVING TO DO THAT TO YOURSELF.
CUTE?
DO YOU ALWAYS GO TO THE MOVIES BY YOURSELF?
YEAH.
GOOD THING I GOT IN SHAPE.
UM...
I'M A FILM GEEK.
I DON'T KNOW WHY, BUT I LOVE GOING TO THE MOVIES ALONE...

YEAH... I UNDERSTAND.
ME, TOO.
WELL, I'D BETTER GET GOING...
YOU SEEM LIKE YOU'RE FEELING BETTER NOW.
UM!
I DON'T KNOW HOW TO THANK YOU...
DON'T WORRY ABOUT IT.
BUT I WOULD GO TO A MOVIE WITH YOU...♡
BESIDES, IT'S GETTING LATE. BE CAREFUL GOING HOME.
HE WAS COOL...
AND NICE...
AND RESPECTFUL.
TOTALLY PERFECT!!
UM...
I WORK AT A RESTAURANT DOWN THE STREET!

IF YOU WANT, COME IN SOMETIME.
I OWE YOU ONE.
TWO WEEKS LATER...
I WAITED AND WONDERED, WHILE GOING ON WITH MY DAILY LIFE, BUT HE STILL DIDN'T SHOW UP.
I COULD ONLY THINK OF ONE THING...
I WONDER IF I'LL EVER SEE HIM AGAIN.
HOW WOULD I EVER FIND HIM?
IF ONLY I'D AT LEAST ASKED HIS NAME.
I NEED JUNK FOOD!
Waaaa
MAYBE YOU WERE HALLUCINATING FROM OVER-DIETING.
THERE'S NO WAY THERE WOULD BE SUCH A PERFECT GUY IN THE REAL WORLD.
IF THERE WERE, I'D BE REALLY SUSPICIOUS.
FOR-GET ABOUT IT.
THAT'S WHY, ON THAT DAY...
WHEN I GOT OFF WORK AND LEFT THE RESTAU-RANT...
AND I SAW HIM STANDING THERE, WAITING FOR ME...
I TOTALLY FELL, HEAD-OVER-HEELS...
IN LOVE WITH HIM.

I NOTICED RIGHT AWAY...
THAT HE HAD A WEDDING RING ON HIS FINGER...
BUT I SOMEHOW IGNORED IT.
IF I HAD TO PINPOINT THE MOMENT WHEN I BLOSSOMED INTO A WOMAN ...
IT WAS RIGHT THEN.
I HAD GENUINELY FALLEN IN LOVE WITH HIM...
AND I BELIEVED THAT HE LOVED ME BACK.

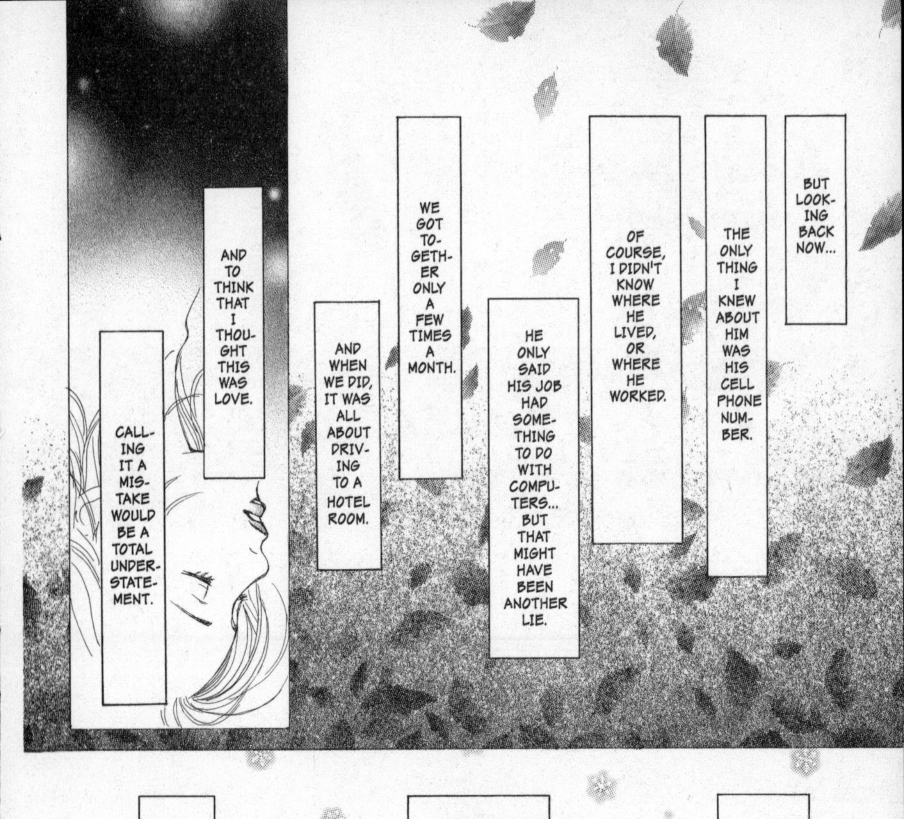

BUT LOOKING BACK NOW...
THE ONLY THING I KNEW ABOUT HIM WAS HIS CELL PHONE NUMBER.
OF COURSE, I DIDN'T KNOW WHERE HE LIVED, OR WHERE HE WORKED.
HE ONLY SAID HIS JOB HAD SOMETHING TO DO WITH COMPUTERS... BUT THAT MIGHT HAVE BEEN ANOTHER LIE.
WE GOT TOGETHER ONLY A FEW TIMES A MONTH.
AND WHEN WE DID, IT WAS ALL ABOUT DRIVING TO A HOTEL ROOM.
AND TO THINK THAT I THOUGHT THIS WAS LOVE.
CALLING IT A MISTAKE WOULD BE A TOTAL UNDERSTATEMENT.

IF IT HAD KEPT GOING ON LIKE THIS...

THERE'S NO DOUBT THAT MY INNOCENCE WOULD HAVE BEEN GROUND OUT OF ME MORE AND MORE.

IT WAS A BLESSING THAT WE BROKE UP.

THIS IS WHAT I TOLD MYSELF, AND TRIED TO GET ON WITH MY LIFE.

MY PLAN IS TO ENROLL IN THE LOCAL ART SCHOOL THIS SPRING WITH MY BEST FRIEND JUN.

THE ART SCHOOL IS CO-ED...

SO MAYBE I'LL FINALLY GET A CHANCE TO MEET SOMEONE SPECIAL.

VALEDICTORIAN, NANA KOMATSU.

NARUSE ART SCHOOL
NANA...
ARE YOU SAYING THAT YOU'RE JUST HERE TO FIND A BOYFRIEND?
......

OF COURSE NOT, JUN. I WANT TO STUDY ART SERIOUSLY, SO...
SEE, MY CLOTHES ARE TOTALLY CASUAL.
THAT'S GOOD.
NO MAT-TER HOW YOU SLICE IT, THERE'S NO WAY YOU'RE GETTING A GUY WITH THAT HAIRDO ANYWAY.
NO SEX AP-PEAL.
YOU DIDN'T HAVE TO SLUM IT THAT MUCH.
gab
gab
gab
HEY!
ISONO SAID IT WAS SUPER CUTE AND GAVE ME RAVE REVIEWS!
WHO THE HECK IS ISONO?
IS HIS FIRST NAME MASUO?
HE'S THE STYLIST WHO DID MY HAIR. ♡
....
WHAT DO YOU WANT ME TO DO?
YOU CAN DO WHATEVER YOU WANT. ♡
....
OOH, THAT GUY...
BUT APPAR-ENTLY ISONO IS MARRIED.
AND HE'S ONLY 21, TOO.
HE SURE RUSHED INTO THINGS.
DUH
OH WELL, I GUESS THAT TAKES CARE OF THAT.
UH-HUH-HH.
NOT THAT IT EVER STOPPED YOU.
JUN!!
YOU PROMISED YOU WOULDN'T TALK ABOUT THAT!

I KNOW I'M LIKE THAT, BUT I'M ACTUALLY TRYING TO REPENT.
I THINK I'VE BEEN CURSED BY THE DEMON LORD...
BECAUSE I WAS WITH ANOTHER WOMAN'S HUSBAND.
THE DEMON LORD ?
AND I REALIZED ANOTHER MAJOR THING...
AREN'T ALL THE PEOPLE I'VE HIT ON OLDER THAN ME?
IT'S NOT LIKE I HAVE AN ELECTRA COMPLEX OR ANY-THING.
THAT'S THE MAJOR ISSUE?
MAYBE MY RELA-TION-SHIPS WENT BAD BECAUSE THE MEN WERE TOO OLD.
THERE'S LOTS OF PEOPLE MY AGE AT THIS SCHOOL...
IF WE'RE THE SAME AGE, THEN WE'D LIKE THE SAME THINGS, AND WE'D BE ABLE TO UNDERSTAND EACH OTHER.
I HAVE THE FEELING A WON-DERFUL ROMANCE COULD HATCH HERE. ♡
SHE IS SO HERE TO GET A GUY.
OH, HERE'S ROOM B-3.
ANYWAY, WHY DON'T YOU JUST STOP FALLING ALL OVER GUYS, NANA?
WHY DON'T YOU WAIT TO FIND OUT THE TRUE NATURE OF THE NEXT PERSON BEFORE...
HEY, ARE YOU LISTENING TO ME?

MY EYES...
... MET WITH HIS.
A BOY WITH SUCH BEAU-TIFUL EYES.
HUH?
WHAT?
WHY?
HE'S WALK-ING RIGHT UP TO ME...

JUN-KO!
IT'S JUNKO, RIGHT?
SHOJI?
YEAH, SHOJI!
WOW, YOU GREW YOUR HAIR OUT, I DIDN'T RECOGNIZE YOU.
....
WOW, IT'S BEEN FOREVER!
IT'S BEEN, LIKE, THREE YEARS SINCE WE GRADUATED FROM JUNIOR HIGH.
BUT ANYWAY, WHY ARE YOU HERE?
AND IN THE SAME CLASS TO BOOT!
UH-OH ...
WHAT?!
I'VE GOT ANOTHER LOUD-MOUTH WITH ME.
I HATE THIS.
JUN...
TO THINK SHE HAD AN ACE LIKE THIS HIDDEN UP HER SLEEVE...
SO THAT'S WHY SHE'S SO BLASÉ AND NEVER GOES OUT WITH ANYONE.
HEY.
IS THIS YOUR FRIEND?
IS SHE A GOS-SIP?
YEP.
MY INSEPAR-ABLE SIDEKICK FROM THE ALL-GIRL HIGH SCHOOL.
SHE'S THE QUEEN OF GOSSIP!
GULP
WHAT'S YOUR NAME?
I'M NANA KOMA-TSU.
OPEN-FOR-BUSINESS SMILE
NICE TO MEET YOU.

I'M SHOJI ENDO.
NICE TO MEET YOU, TOO. ♡
HIS SMILE IS ALSO AMAZ-ING. ♡
......
YOU GUYS SHOULD SIT OVER THERE WITH US.
I'M WITH A BUDDY OF MINE FROM HIGH SCHOOL, TOO.
SWOON
I'LL INTRO-DUCE YOU TO HIM.
NICE TO MEET YOU...
I'M KYOSUKE TAKAKURA.
......
AND HE'S NICE, TOO. ♡
HIS HAIR'S KINDA WEIRD ...
BUT IT LOOKS PRETTY GOOD ON HIM
THIS IS THE OPENING ACT OF HAPPY CAMPUS LIFE, ISN'T IT JUN? ♡
201
Junko Saotome

WHAT DO YOU MEAN CAMPUS LIFE?
IT'S NOT LIKE WE'RE UNIVERSITY STUDENTS...
IT'S A TECHNICAL SCHOOL.
I'M SORRY...
I JUST GET SO EXCITED...
BUT IT'S OKAY, I UNDERSTAND.
SHOJI IS YOUR ACE-IN-THE-HOLE, RIGHT?
DON'T WORRY, I WON'T STEAL HIM FROM YOU.
ACE-IN-THE-HOLE?
YOU JUST DON'T GET IT, DO YOU?
I'M JUST ANNOYED BY YOUR SUDDEN LACK OF INTEGRITY. AND, BY THE WAY, SHOJI AND I ARE JUST FRIENDS.
YOU LIAR!
YOU'LL BE CURSED BY THE DEMON LORD.
IF YOU WERE IN THE SAME CLASS AS A BOY THAT GOOD LOOKING, YOU'D TOTALLY FALL IN LOVE WITH HIM!
IT'S NOT FAIR!
I'M NOT LIKE YOU!
IN JUNIOR HIGH, I HAD A BUNCH OF MALE FRIENDS AND I DIDN'T FALL IN LOVE WITH THEM ONE AFTER ANOTHER.
BESIDES, WHAT PART OF SHOJI DO YOU THINK IS GOOD LOOKING?
A BUNCH OF MALE FRIENDS...
SO THAT'S IT... THAT MUST'VE BEEN NICE.
YOU HAVE TO ADMIRE THAT...
NOW THAT I THINK OF IT, I HAVEN'T HAD A SINGLE MALE FRIEND UP UNTIL NOW.
I WONDER WHY?
WELL, INSTEAD OF SEEING THEM AS HUMANS, YOU ONLY SEE MEN, MEN, MEN. THAT'S WHY.
SO THAT'S IT...
OOOHHH
I HAVE TO THINK OF THEM AS JUST HUMAN...

ALL RIGHT, THAT'S IT!
I'M GOING TO MAKE SHOJI AND KYOSUKE MY MALE FRIENDS.
HUH?
YOU MAKE FRIENDS AS A CONSCIOUS DECISION?
SHOULDN'T IT JUST HAPPEN NATURALLY?
BUT IF I DON'T CONSCIOUSLY DECIDE THAT WE'RE JUST FRIENDS...
I MIGHT SLIP AND FALL IN LOVE.
IF YOU FALL IN LOVE, YOU FALL IN LOVE. IT JUST HAPPENS.
BUT, IN YOUR CASE, IT MIGHT BE A GOOD EXPERIENCE TO TRY TO JUST BE FRIENDS WITH THE BOYS FIRST.
THANKS, JUN! I'M REALLY GOING TO TRY AND DO IT RIGHT THIS TIME!
......
DO WHAT?
RING
RING
RRRINGGGG
I GOTTA ANSWER MY PHONE.
LEMME GO!
HELLO?
OH...
SHOJI?
...
THUMP
THUMP
OKAY, CALM DOWN.
REMEMBER...
HE'S JUST A FRIEND.
UH-HUH, SURE.
WE'RE TOTALLY OPEN.
SO COME OVER TO MY PLACE.
YEAH, NANA'S HERE, TOO.
THUD
OH... AND GET SOME BEER.
AND SOME SNACKS!

HEY GUYS!
BEER
HELLO.
WOW! NICE PLACE.
YOU'RE A TOWNIE, BUT YOU LIVE HERE ALONE? TALK ABOUT GLAMOROUS.
YOU SHOULD BE PUNISH-ED.
THAT'S BECAUSE MY FAM-ILY'S HOME IS REALLY FAR FROM SCHOOL.
UUHHHH
I LIVE FAR AWAY, TOO.
OVER THE HILLS AND THROUGH THE WOODS.
HEH-HEH...
THAT'S BECAUSE SHOJI WOULD GET LONELY LIVING AWAY FROM HIS GRAND-MOTHER.
YEAH, ACTU-ALLY.
KYOSUKE, WHERE DO YOU LIVE?
AROUND HERE.
PLOP
TWITCH
REALLY? WHERE AROUND HERE?
....
BEHIND THE MINI-MART.
....
WOW, YOU REALLY ARE CLOSE. IS IT LIKE A FIVE-MINUTE WALK?
YOU'RE BEING KINDA QUIET NANA.
I THOUGHT YOU'RE SUPPOSED TO BE A LOUD-MOUTH...
ARE YOU BEING SHY?
NO.
FRIENDS! FRIENDS!
THAT AIN'T IT AT ALL.

....
I'M NOT SURE HOW TO TALK TO A MALE FRIEND.
OH NO!
MORE POLITE-LY OR DIRECT OR ROWDY OR WHAT?
.....
AH, DO YOU HAVE A HARD TIME TALKING TO GUYS SOME-TIMES BE-CAUSE YOU WENT TO AN ALL-GIRL HIGH SCHOOL?
BLUSH
IT'S COOL, MAN. LET'S ALL JUST SPILL OUR GUTS AND REALLY GET TO KNOW EACH OTHER.
HEH ...
A CON-FESSION COMPE-TITION? COULD BE SCARY.
IF THEY'RE MY FRIENDS, I SHOULD BE ABLE TO OPEN UP TO THEM...
THAT'S TRUE ...
IT'S HARD MAKING FRIENDS.
HAH !
THAT'S NOT THE CASE AT ALL, RIGHT?
HMMM.
NANA EVEN HAD A BOYFRIEND UP UNTIL RECENTLY.
JUN!!
WHOA
BUT FIRST ...
LET'S HAVE A TOAST!
I BETTER HURRY UP AND GET DRUNK...
SO I CAN LOOSEN UP A LITTLE.
SO THEN...
THE NEXT PERSON I INSTANTLY FELL IN LOVE WITH...
WAS THE PIZZA DELIVERY MAN, "BABY-FACE YOSHIDA"!

AH-HAHA!
BABY-FACE YOSHIDA!
HE WAS SO CUTE! ♡
HIS SMILE! SUPER BABY-FACE!
EEK! ♡
HAHAHAHAHA
AARGH!
YOU TWO, SHUT UP!
YOU'RE DRUNK.
HA HA HA!
TOO FUNNY!
NANA, YOU'RE AWESOME!
NANA! YOU CAN'T DRINK ANYMORE!
glug glug
HEY, IT'S ALL RIGHT. IT'S ENTERTAINING.
HA HA HA
HEH HEH HEH.
SO I JUST KEPT ON ORDERING PIZZAS, I GAINED LIKE 10 POUNDS, AND THEN HE NEVER CAME BACK TO MY HOUSE.
BIG FAT LOSS!
SO THEN WHAT?
WHO WAS THE NEXT GUY?
THE NEXT GUY WAS... ♡
HAHAHA!
SERIOUSLY, THERE'S MORE?

HA HA HA
THE NEXT PERSON...
WAS SOMEONE WHOSE NAME I DIDN'T EVEN KNOW.

I...
DIDN'T THINK I'D EVER SEE YOU AGAIN.
I DIDN'T EVEN...
ASK YOU YOUR NAME....

TAKASHI...
ASANO.
STOP ...

THAT NAME ...
WAS PROBABLY MADE UP ANYWAY.
NANA ...
KTAK
A SAPPY DRUNK ?
HEY HEY, WHAT'S WRONG ?
NANA ...
NO!!
Yank
NANA !
......
NO?
SORRY SHOJI !
DON'T WORRY ABOUT HER !
I AM WORRIED.
OH NANA, YOU DRANK WAY TOO MUCH.
JUN ...
DON'T ...
TOUCH ME.

YOU DON'T LOVE ME...
DON'T TOUCH ME.
NNNN
NNNN
Creak
JUNKO.

KYOSUKE PASSED OUT...
IS IT OKAY TO LEAVE HIM LYING AROUND HERE?
YEAH...
NO PROB-LEM.
SNORE
SOR-RY...
WHEN HE WAKES UP, HE'LL PROB-ABLY JUST GET UP AND LEAVE ON HIS OWN.
......
I'M GON-NA TAKE OFF NOW...
OR I'LL MISS THE LAST TRAIN.
OH, THAT'S RIGHT, YOU'RE WAY OUT THERE.
WHY DON'T YOU JUST SPEND THE NIGHT?
I HAVE TWO ROOMS.
NO, THAT'S ALL RIGHT.
IT'S JUST THAT...
HEY, SHOJI...
YOU DON'T HAVE A GIRL-FRIEND, RIGHT?
HAVE YOU FALLEN IN LOVE WITH ME, JUNKO?
....
WHAT'S WITH THE FACE?!
MAN, YOU NEVER OPENED UP, EVEN BACK IN THE DAY.
WHEN I WAS IN HIGH SCHOOL, I HAD 5 TO 10 GIRL-FRIENDS, TOO.
I WOULDA LOVED TO SHOW YOU A GOOD TIME BACK THEN.

I JUST SO HAPPEN TO NOT HAVE A GIRLFRIEND RIGHT NOW.
SNICKER
SNICKER ?
I THOUGHT NOT.
YOU CAME HERE TONIGHT BECAUSE OF NANA, DIDN'T YOU?
YOU'VE ALWAYS BEEN SO EASY TO READ.
....
BUT NANA SAID SHE DIDN'T LIKE ME?
WHEN SHE SAID "NO"...
I DON'T THINK SO.
FROM THE MOMENT NANA FIRST SAW YOU, SHE'S BEEN SAYING "DREAMY" ♡ AND "SO COOL." ♡
NO WAY
WELL, BEST OF LUCK TO YA.
PAT
WHAT THE HELL IS THAT?
DON'T YOU HAVE A KIND BONE IN YOUR BODY TO SAY "I'LL HELP YOU OUT" OR SOMETHING?!
chirp...
CLICK

......
WHERE AM I?
STAB
!!
MY HEAD HUUURRRTTTS!!
WHAT THE HELL IS THIS?
pound pound pound
IT'S LIKE ARMA-GED-DON!
OH YEAH, LAST NIGHT ...
SHOJI AND KYOSUKE BROUGHT US BEER...
WE TOASTED, DRANK LIKE FISH, GOT WILD AND CRAZY AND...
RAH RAH
....
I CAN'T REALLY REMEM-BER, BUT I THINK I HAD A GREAT TIME. ♡
MALE FRIENDS ARE GREAT, AREN'T THEY!
OH, MAN...
IT'S ALREADY LIGHT OUT.
I DIDN'T CALL HOME YET.
UH-OH
pound pound pound
JUNNN ...
click
DO YOU HAVE ANY ASPI-RIN?

WHOOSH
SKRCH
EVE
頭痛薬
WELL, YOU KNOW, UH, YEAH...
WE WERE JUST TALKING ALL NIGHT, AND THEN I GUESS WE REALLY HIT IT OFF.

AND SO, WE WERE JUST...
WHY IS SHE MAKING EXCUS-ES?
I DIDN'T KNOW WHAT I WAS DOING...
NO, FROM THE MOMENT I FIRST SAW JUNKO, I THOUGHT SHE WAS REALLY COOL.
BLUSH
CLUNK

WELL PUT, KYOSUKE.
GOOD FOR YOU!
FALLING IN LOVE ISN'T ABOUT LOGIC!
THAT'S TRUE NANA, YOU'RE THE EXPERT ON LOVE AT FIRST SIGHT.
HA HA HA!
HUH?
EXPERT?
HOW WOULD YOU KNOW??
JUNKO, YOU BLABBER MOUTH!
YOU'RE THE ONE WHO BLABBED IT, REMEMBER?
REALLY ...??
click
click
click
click
MAN, LOOK WHAT TIME IT IS.
I GOTTA GO HOME AND CHANGE, THEN GO TO SCHOOL.
CLATTER
NANA, YOU'LL BE LATE IF YOU GO HOME FIRST.
DO YOU WANNA BORROW SOME CLOTHES?
AND I CALLED YOUR HOUSE LAST NIGHT...
I TOLD THEM YOU HAD A STOMACHACHE AND COULDN'T MOVE SO YOU'D BE STAYING HERE.
MAKE SURE YOUR STORY MATCHES UP.
ARE YOU LISTENING TO ME?
BLABBED...
click click click
HOW MUCH DID I TELL AND WHAT DID I SAY...
YOU STARTED WITH OKAMOTO FROM ART CLASS.
THEN NAKAMURA FROM THE VIDEO STORE.
KAWASAKI THE COOK...
YOSHIDA FROM THE PIZZA PLACE.
YOU TALKED ABOUT EVERYTHING IN A FUNNY AND WEIRD WAY.
OH NO...

BUT, NANA...
WITH TAKASHI...
YOU STILL HAVEN'T FORGOTTEN ABOUT HIM, HAVE YOU?
BUT THAT'S NO SURPRISE.
NOT AT ALL, I TOTALLY FORGOT ABOUT THAT POSER!
TO THE POINT OF TELLING FUNNY STORIES ABOUT HIM TO OTHER PEOPLE!
NO, YOU WERE CRYING.
WHEN IT CAME TO HIM, YOU STARTED CRYING AND DIDN'T TELL THE STORY.

HEY, NANA!
IF YOU THINK YOU MIGHT LIKE SHOJI...
I'LL HELP YOU OUT. ♡
JUN ...?
WHAT GIVES, ALL OF A SUDDEN...
TALKING ALL NICE AND CUTESY.
DO YOU FEEL THAT GUILTY ABOUT GETTING TOGETHER WITH KYOSUKE?
NO, I'M SO SURE!

SHOJI'S A REALLY GOOD GUY.
I THINK HE'D BE VERY LOYAL WITH A GIRL-FRIEND.
HE'D BE VERY GOOD TO YOU NANA.
I GUARAN-TEE IT.
JUNNN. ♡
IF YOU WERE A GUY, JUN, I'D TOTALLY BE YOUR GIRLFRIEND. ♡
HA! I WOULDN'T!
NOT WITH YOU.
SERI-OUSLY!
BUT IT'S OKAY. I'VE BECOME FRIENDS WITH SHOJI, SO...
HUH?
SHOJI'S A VERY IMPOR-TANT MALE FRIEND, YA KNOW?
IT WOULD TAKE SOME TIME BEFORE HE COULD BE SOME-THING LIKE A BOY-FRIEND.
SOME-THING LIKE A BOY-FRIEND?
A MALE FRIEND IS BETTER THAN A BOY-FRIEND?
JUNKO...
NANA...

MORNIN'!
OH, GOOD ...
YOU SEEM GOOD, NANA.
I'M SUPER GOOD. ♡
I WAS REALLY HUNG-OVER, BUT I TOOK SOME ASPIRIN, SO IT'S BETTER.
WHEN DID YOU LEAVE LAST NIGHT SHOJI?
......
WELL I GUESS YOU'RE DOING JUST FINE...
WITH THE LAST TRAIN.
I CAN'T GO TO BED WITHOUT HEARING MY GRAND-MOTHER'S LULLABY.
AH HA HA!!
SERI-OUSLY?
WELL, I GUESS IT'S ALL RIGHT.
WHAT-EVER WILL BE, WILL BE.
SNIP
A MOVIE?
YEAH.
YOU SAID YOU LIKED MOVIES YESTER-DAY, DIDN'T YOU?
......
IF YOU'RE FREE THIS SUNDAY, DO YOU WANNA GO SEE A MOVIE WITH ME?
SORRY.
AS A RULE, I ONLY WATCH MOVIES BY MYSELF.
I DON'T KNOW IF IT'S BECAUSE I'D BE DIS-TRACTED BY HAVING A FRIEND SIT NEXT TO ME OR WHAT...

......
A FRIEND ...?
THIS IS POINT-LESS.
......
YEAH, I UNDERSTAND.
ME, TOO.
SNIP
NURSE
OW!
WHAT THE HELL WERE YOU DOING...
A COMPO-SITION IN BLOOD?
SPLASH
Antiseptic

Waaaa
IT HURTS!
DEMON LORD. PLEASE RE-LEASE ME!
THE DEMON LORD OF TER-ROR.
I'M CURSED BY HIM...
DEMON LORD?
WHAT THE HELL IS THAT?
YOU'RE JUST A KLUTZ.
HERE, PUT YOUR HAND OUT.
!
OWW!! STOP IT! IT STINGS!!
WAAAA
YOU HAVE TO DO THIS!
YOU CRY-BABY!
IF YOU DON'T, IT'LL GET INFECTED AND HURT MORE AND MORE, YA KNOW?
IS THAT WHAT YOU WANT?
IF I DON'T TAKE CARE OF IT, IT WILL BECOME MORE AND MORE...
YOU STILL HAVEN'T FORGOTTEN ABOUT TAKASHI, HAVE YOU?
NOT ONLY CAN I NOT FORGET ABOUT HIM...
IT'S AN OPEN WOUND, JUN.

THE MORE TIME THAT GOES BY...

THE MORE I THINK OF HIM.

HIS EVERY SINGLE MOVE.

IT ALL SEEMS TO HAVE BEEN A LIE, AND I FEEL LIKE I'M GOING TO DIE FROM THE PAIN.

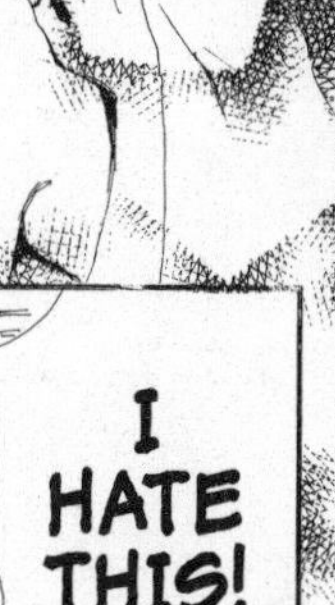

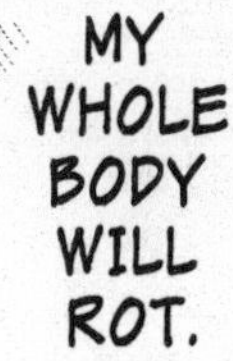

IF I GO ON LIKE THIS...

MY WHOLE BODY WILL ROT.

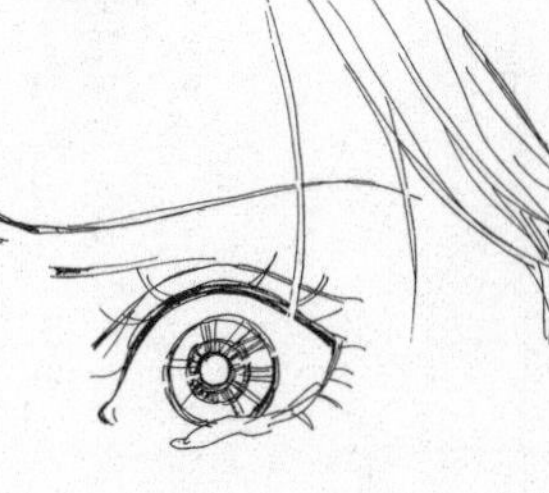

THANK YOU...
YOU'RE REALLY NICE, SHOJI.
IT WAS NOTHING...
WELL, MAYBE A LITTLE...
HEY, SHOJI...
DO YOU THINK YOU COULD MEND A BROKEN HEART?
...A HEART...?
I DON'T KNOW...
I THINK... THE ONLY WAY IS FOR ME TO FALL IN LOVE AGAIN.
SO, WHAT DO YOU THINK?

....
I THINK YOU'RE RIGHT.
NANA...

ALL RIGHT, THEN!
JUMP
SHOJI...
WHERE DO YOU THINK IS THE HIPPEST PLACE IN TOWN FOR KIDS MY AGE TO HANG OUT AT?
KIDS?
...
TEENS WHO DON'T WEAR SUITS!
RIGHT!
?
...LIKE THE ARCADE?
NO, NO...
THAT'S JUST GOT LITTLE BRATS AND OLD MEN.
BE-SIDES, IT'S NOT COOL.
THEN I GUESS THERE MUST BE SOME CLUB.
BINGO!!
?
I MUST FALL IN LOVE...
HEAPS AND HEAPS AND HEAPS OF LOVE.
TO-NIGHT, LET'S ALL GO OUT TO A CLUB.
JUN!
??
SURE... IS YOUR HAND ALL RIGHT?
IF YOU WANNA GO TO A CLUB, THERE'S A GOOD PLACE CLOSE TO HERE.

AND I'LL BANISH MY PATHETIC FORMER SELF TO DARKNESS.
CLUB
Cosmic Connection
B1
CREAK...
NANA.

YOU WERE HERE ALL THIS TIME?
OOOHHHH! ♡ DJ MATSUSHITA IS SO COOL!
SUPER FOXY! SUPER CHILL!
EEK♡
IF YOU LIKE HIM SO MUCH, WHY DON'T YOU TELL HIM?
IF YOU'RE LUCKY, MAYBE HE'LL GO OUT WITH YOU, YA KNOW?

BUT I DON'T WANT THAT.
MATSUSHITA IS A LADIES' MAN AND SUPPOSEDLY A TOTAL PLAYER.
RUMOR HAS IT, HE GOES THROUGH THE LADIES ONE RIGHT AFTER THE OTHER.
HE'S NO GOOD.
AN ENEMY OF WOMEN!
THEN JUST DON'T FALL FOR HIM.

HEY! THAT ADVICE SOUNDS FAMILIAR.
SHOJI, YOU'RE TURNING INTO JUN.
MAYBE I'LL JUST CALL YOU SHO-JUN FROM NOW ON.
ANYONE WOULD GET THAT WAY AFTER HANGING AROUND YOU!
BUT JUN DOESN'T TREAT ME THE WAY SHE USED TO.
SHE'S TOTALLY IN LOVE WITH KYOSUKE, AND IT'S SOFTENED HER... OR TONED HER DOWN A BIT.
SHE'S LOST HER EDGE.

BUT IT'S COOL, MAN. ♡
I HAVE YOU NOW, SHOJI!
AFTER ALL, I'M JUST JUNKO'S REPLACEMENT.
ANYWAY, SHO-JUN, IS THERE A REASON YOU CAME LOOKING FOR ME?
I WAS IN THE BASEMENT, SO MY CELL PHONE DIDN'T RING. SORRY.
DON'T CALL ME SHO-JUN.
I WAS DRINKING AT A BAR IN FRONT OF THE TRAIN STATION WITH KYOSUKE AND THEM, SO I THOUGHT I'D INVITE YOU.
YOU WOULD SAY WE DITCHED YOU, IF I DIDN'T COME FIND YOU.
YAY! ♡
I'LL GO, LET'S GO!
LET'S DRINK, LET'S DRINK!
MAN, IT'S LIKE ALL WE EVER DO IS DRINK.
AREN'T THERE ANY OTHER CLUBS OR ANYTHING?
I WANNA GO TO THE BEACH FOR A CHANGE.
I MEAN, IT IS SUMMER.
HEY, IT'S ALMOST SUMMER VACATION. LET'S ALL GO SOMEWHERE ON A TRIP OR SOMETHING!
THE BEACH !!

SPLASH

AHHH♡H!
I LOVE THE OCEAN.
IT MAKES ME FEEL YOUNG AND HAPPY.
DRINKING, OF COURSE.
I WAS SO BORED OF SEEING JUST MOUNTAINS ALL THE TIME.
Sea Side hotel
HEH HEH!
I'M DEFINITELY SICK OF LOOKING AT MOUNTAINS.
yawn
I'M TIRED.
OH REALLY, JUN? ♡
THEN WE SHALL BID YOU FAREWELL.
WHAT ARE YOU TALKING ABOUT, NANA? THIS IS YOUR ROOM.
MAN, ARE YOU DRUNK ALREADY?
I'LL GIVE IT UP TO JUN AND KYOSUKE. ♡
I'LL SLEEP WITH YOU, SHOJI.
WHaa?!
WHAT ARE YOU SAYING ...?
UGH... GOD, AREN'T YOU FRIENDLY, SHOJI!
LET'S HURRY UP AND GO.
HEY.
.....
SLAM
THEY SEEM TO BE GETTING ALONG JUST FINE WITHOUT US.
WELL, HELL.
YOU THINK IT'S GONNA BE THAT EASY?

WHAT THE HELL ARE YOU THINKING?
IT'S COOL, MAN. THERE'S TWO BEDS, AND I WON'T ASSAULT YOU, SO DON'T WORRY. ♡
IF YOU WANT, I'LL SING YOU A LULLABY LIKE YOUR GRAND-MOTHER.
YOU DON'T HAVE TO SING TO ME!
EVEN IF YOU'RE COOL, I'M NOT.
I MIGHT JUMP ON YOU!
WHY ...?
WHAT DO YOU MEAN "WHY?"
WE'RE FRIENDS, RIGHT?
....
NANA ...
YOU REALLY DON'T KNOW SQUAT ABOUT HOW MEN REALLY ARE.
GUYS CAN DO IT EVEN WHEN THEY'RE NOT IN LOVE!

I KNOW THAT...
BUT I THOUGHT YOU WERE DIFFER-ENT, SHOJI...
JUN TOLD ME SO...
I'M SORRY TO SAY IT, BUT THAT'S HOW I AM!
I DON'T KNOW WHAT JUNKO TOLD YOU, BUT...
BECAUSE I REALLY LIKED YOU SHOJI... AND NOW I'M BUMMED AT YOU!
WHY ARE YOU CRYING?

NO, YOU KNOW HOW IT IS, NANA...
WHEN YOU SAY "REALLY LIKE"...
DO YOU MEAN "AS A FRIEND"?
YEAH, OF COURSE.
I LIKE YOU AS A HUMAN, NOT JUST AS A MEMBER OF THE MALE SPECIES!
SHOJI, YOU'RE MY MOST IMPORTANT MALE FRIEND, MORE THAN ANYONE ELSE!
MALE SPECIES?
BUT YOU'RE RIGHT.
SHOJI, YOU'RE STILL A MEMBER OF THE MALE SPECIES, AND IT MIGHT BE DANGEROUS FOR US TO SLEEP IN THE SAME ROOM.
I WAS WRONG.
IT'S HARD TO MAINTAIN A CO-ED FRIENDSHIP, ISN'T IT SHO-JUN?
....
BUT LET'S TRY OUR BEST!
WELL, I'M GOING BACK TO MY ROOM.
WAIT, NANA!
THAT MIGHT BE BAD!
THEY MIGHT BE A LITTLE, UH, BUSY!
JUMP
OH, YEAH.
WHAT TO DO...
I WONDER WHEN THEY'LL BE DONE.
......
...YOU REALLY SHOULDN'T BE ASKING ME...
IT DEPENDS, YA KNOW.
WHAT A PREDICAMENT.
IT MIGHT BE WEIRD, YOU KNOW, IF I CALLED THEM ON THE PHONE TO ASK...
......

ALL RIGHT, I GET IT, NANA.
JUST SLEEP IN HERE!
I'LL SLEEP OVER ON THAT BED.
GOOD NIGHT.
YOU CAN'T SHOJI! IT'S DANGER-OUS!
NOTH-ING TO WORRY ABOUT NOW!
WHY NOT?
WELL, YOU JUST SAID I BUMMED YOU OUT, DIDN'T YOU?
I WOULDN'T WANT TO DO ANY MORE OF THAT!
BE-CAUSE OF OUR FRIEND-SHIP.

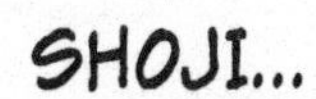
SHOJI...

I LOVE YOU! ♡
ROCK-A-BYE BA-BY
YOU DON'T HAVE TO SING TO ME!!

AHAHAHAHA

IT'S NOTHING TO LAUGH ABOUT. UGH.
I DIDN'T GET A BIT OF SLEEP.
IF I GO IN THE WATER TODAY, I'LL PROB-ABLY DIE.
A JOB WELL DONE, SHO-JUN. ♡
DON'T CALL ME SHO-JUN.
I CAN GO TO TOKYO NOW WITH SOME PEACE OF MIND.
I'M DEPENDING ON YOU TO BE THERE FOR NANA FROM NOW ON.
YEAH, YEAH.
WE'RE JUST FRIENDS THOUGH.
JUNNNN...
COME SWIMMING!
LET'S SWIM TOGETHER!
CLUNK
ER BEER
BEER
ラガービール
生

YOU'RE GONNA REGRET IT IF YOU SIT OUT FOR TOO LONG.
YOU'RE LOW ON MELANIN YOU KNOW.
KYOSUKE ...
IS JUNKO REALLY GOING TO TOKYO ?
YEAH, YOU HEARD.
WHY ?
WHAT FOR ?
THIS ISN'T JUST FOR A VACA-TION?
SHE'S APPLYING TO ART SCHOOL IN TOKYO NEXT YEAR.
EVEN IF SHE DOESN'T GET IN, SHE'S GONNA GO TO A PREP-SCHOOL IN TOKYO.
APPLY-ING? HELL, IF IT'S JUNKO, SHE'LL ...
BUT IS IT OKAY WITH YOU?
WHY ARE YOU SO CALM ABOUT IT?
WHY? BE-CAUSE ...
splash
I'M GOING, TOO.

NO, NO, NO, NO!
I DON'T WANT YOU TO GO! JUNNNN!
.....
NANA, AREN'T YOU GOING TO STOP ME FROM GOING?
I'M FEELIN' KINDA LEFT OUT HERE.
THAT'S RIGHT!
IF YOU DON'T GO, THEN JUN WON'T GO EITHER, RIGHT?
DON'T GO KYOSUKE!!!
WAAA
.....
UGH... STOP IT RIGHT NOW, NANA!
EVEN IF KYOSUKE DOESN'T GO, I'M GOING ANYWAY!
I REALLY WANT TO STUDY ART IN TOKYO!
YO DUDE, IT'S MY LIFE. YOU'RE NOT THE BOSS OF ME!

...I'M SORRY.
IT'S TRUE.
YOU'RE RIGHT, JUN.
BUT I'LL BE...
LONELY.
MORE LONELY THAN THAT ONE SNOWY DAY...
EVEN SAD-DER.
OH, THAT'S RIGHT...
IT'S JULY, ISN'T IT?

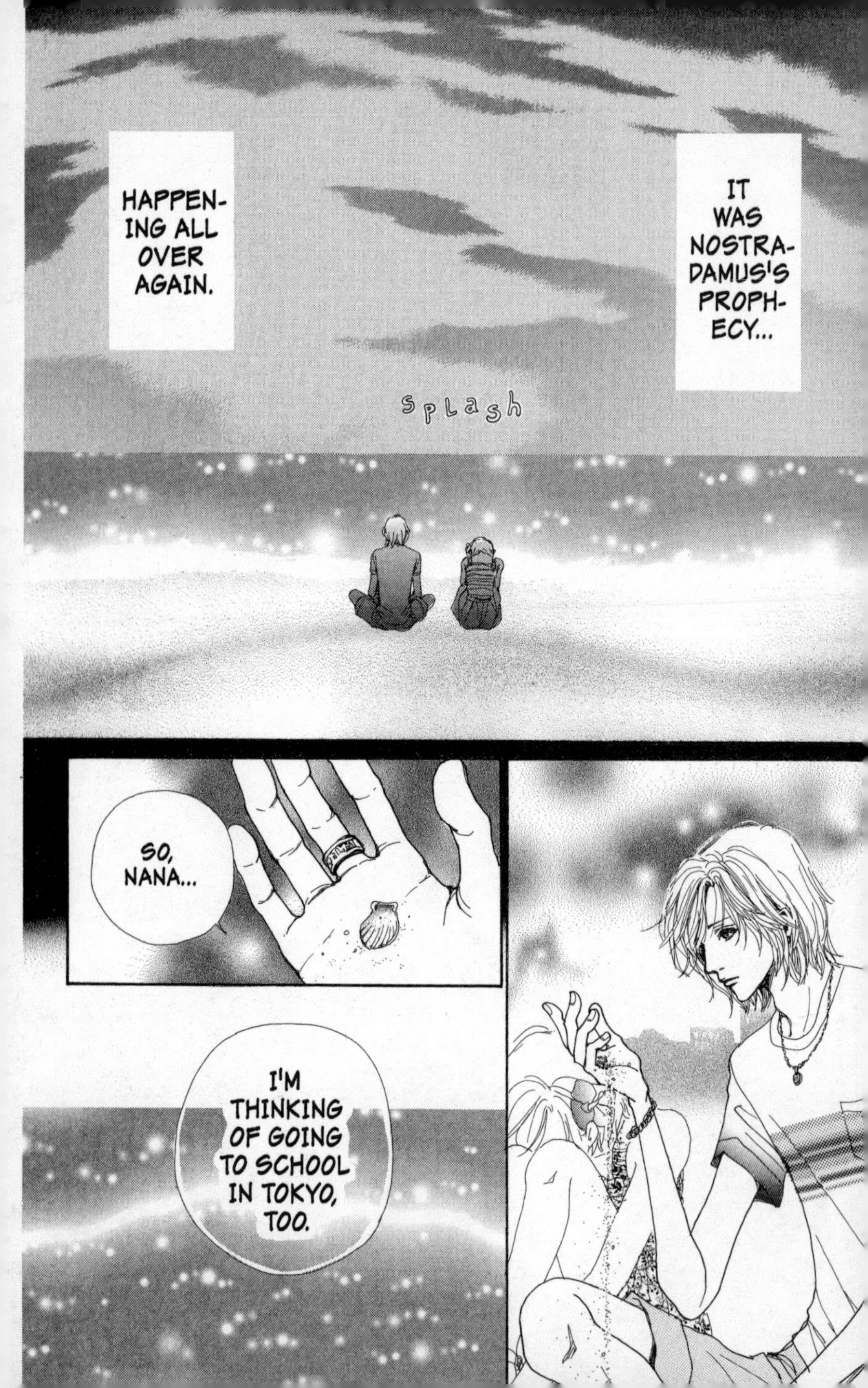
IT WAS NOSTRA-DAMUS'S PROPH-ECY...
HAPPEN-ING ALL OVER AGAIN.
splash
SO, NANA...
I'M THINKING OF GOING TO SCHOOL IN TOKYO, TOO.

MAYBE YOU'D LIKE TO GO WITH ME?

THUD THUD THUD
S ART UNIVERSITY
(Entrance Exam Information)
A Art Schoo
Tokyo M Colleg
of Fine Arts
TOKYO F ART COLLEGE
Information

WOW... THAT'S SO COOL!
TOKYO HAS SO MANY ART SCHOOLS.
WITH THAT MANY SCHOOLS, THEY GOTTA LET ME IN SOME-WHERE!
YEAH, JUST APPLY TO ALL OF 'EM, MAN.
AND IF I DON'T GET IN, I CAN JUST GO TO COMMUNITY COLLEGE FIRST.
.....
WHAT THE HELL ...
WHY WOULD YOU DO THAT?
YO DUDE, IT'S MY LIFE! YOU'RE NOT THE BOSS OF ME!
SMACK
HEY ...
I JUST WANNA GO TO TOKYO WITH ALL YOU GUYS...
JUST DO WHAT YOU WANT.
I DON'T WANNA TELL YOU HOW TO RUN YOUR LIFE.
SLAM

JUNKOOOOO♥
IF I'M "ABANDONING" YOU, WHY ARE YOU SO HAPPY?!
I'LL BE ON MY BEST BEHAVIOR!
NO MORE PARTYING!
I'LL RETIRE FROM CLUB LIFE!
GOOD RIDDANCE, 20-YEAR-OLD DJ MATSUSHITA!
GO MACK ON SOME OTHER CHICK!
Move to Tokyo
DIE Demon Lord
NO Drinking
FORGET ROMANCE... I GOTTA WORK ON GETTING OUTTA HERE!

BESIDES, IF I GO TO TOKYO...
THERE'S TONS OF GREAT PEOPLE...
THERE'S A LOT OF COOL SHOPS...
AND I CAN GET MY HAIR DONE PRO.
EVERYTHING'S PERFECT THERE!

THIS IS THE BEGINNING OF OUR MAGICAL TOKYO ADVENTURES, ISN'T IT JUN?!
FINALLY, SOME REAL CAMPUS LIFE!
Tokyo F Art College
T ART UNIVERSITY
M College of Fine Arts
A Art School
S ART UNIVERSITY

YEAH ...
LIFE DOESN'T FALL INTO PLACE SO EASILY, DOES IT?
WHAT WENT WRONG...? I TRIED SO HARD. I DIDN'T GET IN ANYWHERE... I'M JUST CURSED, THAT'S IT...
DON'T YOU BLAME IT ON YOUR DEMON LORD.
THE DEMON LORD'S CURSE HAS ME NOW, TOO...
HOW'S THIS CURSE CONTA-GIOUS?
WELL, YOU'RE THE LUCKY ONES, JUN! YOU GOT INTO YOUR FIRST CHOICE, AND YOU'LL BE ABLE TO PARTY ALL YOU WANT THIS SPRING.
YEAH... YEAH!
I'M NOT GOING TO COLLEGE TO PARTY!
IT ISN'T FAIR JUN, YOU HAVE ALL THE LUCK!
THE DEMON LORD PLAYS FAVOR-ITES!
....
DON'T INVOLVE ME IN YOUR WEIRD CULT !!
SLAM
BUT Y'KNOW, NANA ...
SO YOU DIDN'T GET INTO A UNIVER-SITY, BUT YOU COULD START OUT AT A COMMUNITY COLLEGE, RIGHT?
MY PARENTS SAID THEY'LL ONLY PAY FOR A UNIVER-SITY...
BUT I DON'T WANNA JUST KEEP TRYING TO GET IN...
WHAT AM I GONNA DO ...?
SO YOU'RE A WANNABE STUDENT COME SPRING, HUH?
WELL, THAT'S ALL RIGHT, TOO.
THAT'S LIFE.

HEY, SORRY 'BOUT THAT, BUT HOW 'BOUT WE START HEADING BACK TO THE HOTEL?
I WANNA GET UP EARLY TOMORROW AND START LOOKING FOR HOUSING.
YEAH.
JUN...
"SORRY 'BOUT THAT"...
WHAT AM I GONNA DO...
......
NANA...
SINCE WE'RE ALREADY HERE IN TOKYO, WANNA GO LOOK AROUND?
YEAH! ♡
I WONDER WHERE'S A GOOD PLACE TO GO...
click click
YOU GUYS GO ON WITHOUT US.
ALL RIGHT.
DON'T GET TOO DRUNK.
THERE'S NO END TO YOUR "RESPONSIBILITIES" THERE.
WOW, TOKYO SEEMS SO... YOU KNOW...
I CAN'T BELIEVE IT'S THIS LATE BUT STILL SO CROWDED.
I FEEL LIKE A TOTAL COUNTRY GIRL.
OOHH AAHH
YOU ARE A TOTAL COUNTRY GIRL.
STOP STARING AT EVERYTHING.
SO ANYWAYS, IN APRIL...
DON'T YOU THINK IT MIGHT BE BEST TO JUST STAY AT THE LOCAL ART SCHOOL?

YEAH, BUT ...
I WANNA MOVE TO TOKYO NO MATTER WHAT.
I FEEL LIKE IT'S MY FAULT.
I'M THE ONE WHO GOT YOU TO MOVE.
MAYBE IT'S BETTER IF YOU STAY BACK HOME.
NO WAY, MAN!
......
DO YOU NEED TO BE WITH JUNKO THAT MUCH?
NOW THAT'S A DOOMED LOVE AFFAIR ...
BUT ...
BUT YOU'RE MOVING TO TOKYO TOO, AREN'T YOU SHOJI?
I'M, WELL ...
YEAH, I'M GONNA ENROLL IN AN S.A.T. SCHOOL HERE ...
AND APPLY TO UNIVERSITY AGAIN NEXT YEAR.
I'M SCREWED ...
THEN I'M MOVING TO TOKYO, TOO!
EVEN IF I CAN'T GET MONEY FROM MY 'RENTS, I'LL WORK ODD JOBS AND PROVE I CAN MAKE IT!
WHAT THE HELL ARE YOU TALKING ABOUT? DON'T GO CRAZY ON ME!
WHAT'S SO CRAZY ABOUT IT?
I'LL BE FINE, I CAN DO IT.
YOU'LL DIE HOMELESS!
YOU DON'T HAVE ENOUGH MONEY TO SURVIVE WITHOUT AN ALLOWANCE.
THAT'S WHY I SAID I'D WORK PART-TIME!

WHAT ABOUT RENT MONEY? YOU'LL NEED HUNDREDS OF THOU-SANDS OF YEN TO START OUT WITH, YA KNOW?
YOU AREN'T A KID ANYMORE, SO AT LEAST ACKNOWL-EDGE THAT.
WHY DON'T YOU GET REAL FOR ONCE?!
THEN I'LL GO TO AN S.A.T. SCHOOL TOO...
AND THEN MY 'RENTS MIGHT GIVE ME SOME MONEY.
WHAT THE HELL?
DON'T JUST GO TO S.A.T. SCHOOL FOR NO REASON.
THEN WHAT SHOULD I...
JUST STAY BACK HOME.
SHOJI, YOU WON'T MISS ME, WILL YOU...
I AIN'T GONNA MISS YOU AT ALL!
I'LL BE LIBER-ATED!
blah
blah
blah

WHAT AM I TO YOU, ANY-WAYS?
YOU LOVE IT, DON'T YOU, PLAYING MY FEELINGS BY GETTING ALL TEARY-EYED AND SAYING THINGS TO GET ME STOKED?
YOU JUST WANT A GUY NEARBY, WHO YOU'RE ONLY NICE TO WHEN IT'S CONVENIENT.

TO HELL WITH YOUR CO-ED FRIEND-SHIP.
DON'T MAKE ME LAUGH.

blah
blah
OHMIGOD!
AH HA HA!
BUMP
blah
blah
blah
blah
blah
blah
blah

blah
blah

BUT I DON'T...

KNOW HOW.

BECAUSE I ALWAYS JUST DEPEND ON SHOJI...

AND DIDN'T NOTICE WHERE WE WERE.

I HAD NO REASON TO WATCH WHERE WE WERE GOING.

AND NOW I'VE HIT ROCK BOTTOM.

I WONDER WHERE I'M EVEN STANDING RIGHT NOW.
NANA?
blah
blah
blah
blah
blah
THAT'S RIGHT.
I'M IN TOKYO.
blah
AND TOKYO...
IS WHERE HE LIVES.
BUT HE COULDN'T REALLY BE...

I THOUGHT IT WAS YOU...
WHAT'S WRONG?
WHAT ARE YOU DOING HERE?
HE FOUND ME...
IN THIS CROWDED CITY.
IT'S OVER.

BUT!
SHE WAS DRIVING ME CRAZY. I JUST LOST IT.
OUR CONVERSATION GOT SO WEIRD!
I UNDERSTAND WHY YOU LOST IT.
OF COURSE YOU WOULD!
BUT I CAN'T BELIEVE YOU JUST DITCHED HER IN THE MIDDLE OF THE CITY LIKE THAT!
WELL...
TAP
AT LEAST THE STREETS ARE WELL LIT, AND THERE'S LOTS OF PEOPLE AROUND.
SHE SHOULD BE ABLE TO FIND HER WAY BACK.
THAT'S NOT THE PROBLEM!
SHUT YOUR MOUTH!
.....
NOW THAT IT'S COME TO THIS, I GOTTA TELL YOU, SHOJI.
NANA'S IN LOVE WITH YOU.
WHAT?
YEAH, RIGHT.
BEFORE YOU WRITE HER OFF, YOU'D BETTER THINK HARD ABOUT HOW MUCH YOU HURT NANA, WHO LOVES YOU, BY TREATING HER THE WAY YOU JUST DID!
SLAM
......

Y'KNOW, I SORTA THOUGHT SO.
......
WHAT-EVER, DUDE.
BUT I THOUGHT MAYBE IT WAS JUST MY EGO.
WELL, IF JUNKO SAYS IT, IT'S PROB-ABLY TRUE, DON'T YA THINK?
RASH
SLAM
......
A CLUE-LESS SEARCH PARTY ...
WHAT A CRAZY CREW.
OH WELL.

REALLY ...
SO YOU APPLIED TO ART SCHOOL HERE.

BUT I FAILED SPECTACULARLY TO GET INTO ANY OF THEM...
I'VE RUN OUT OF OPTIONS.
IT SUCKS 'CAUSE I'VE BEEN TRYING SO HARD TO MOVE TO TOKYO.

OH!
BUT THIS IS DIFFERENT.
IT HAS NOTHING TO DO WITH YOU, TAKASHI. IT'S NOT LIKE I'M CHASING YOU AROUND LIKE FATAL ATTRACTION.
I'M NOT GONNA STALK YOU OR ANYTHING.
DON'T WORRY!

YOU HAVEN'T CHANGED A BIT, NANA.
HUH?
YOU DON'T ...
NOT AT ALL?
LIKE MY HAIR ...
OR MY OUTFIT?
I ACTUALLY THINK I'VE DIGRESSED SINCE HIGH SCHOOL.
I'M SO EMBARRASSED YOU'RE SEEING ME LIKE THIS.
BUT THIS IS MORE YOU, NANA.
I... OH, OKAY.
THE WAY YOU TALK HASN'T CHANGED AT ALL.
"IT'S NOT LIKE I'M CHASING YOU..."
"I'M NOT GONNA STALK YOU OR ANYTHING--"
"DON'T WORRY!"
....

YOU WOULD SAY THAT EVERY TIME WE GOT TO-GETHER.
AND EACH TIME, IT WAS REALLY HARD.

....

FLICK
....
WHY ?

ARGH...
WELL YOU HAVEN'T CHANGED AT ALL EITHER, TAKASHI.
EVERY TIME I ASKED YOU WHAT'S WRONG,YOU NEVER SAID ANY-THING.
HUH ?
YEAH ...
HEH HEH
AND EVERY TIME YOU DIDN'T ANSWER WAS HARD ON ME, YA KNOW?
REALLY ?
I'M SORRY.

THE WEIRD THING IS...
I THOUGHT I COULDN'T STAND THIS GUY.
BUT AFTER SEEING HIM AGAIN, I JUST CAN'T HATE HIM ANY-MORE.
I HAVE TO BELIEVE IT WAS REAL.

I REALLY DID LOVE HIM.
AND HE LOVED ME BACK, EVEN IF FOR A MOMENT.
AND THAT'S OKAY, I SHOULD ACCEPT IT.
I DON'T HAVE TO BEAT MYSELF UP OVER IT.
OH.
NOW I GET IT!
THIS ALL LOOKS FAMILIAR.
JUST GO STRAIGHT DOWN THIS STREET, AND YOU'LL SEE YOUR HOTEL.
OKAY, THANKS.
HEY? MR. ASANO?
WHAT ARE YOU DOING HERE?
AT THIS TIME OF NIGHT ...
AND WHO'S THIS GIRL WITH YOU ?
HM-MM ...
......
I MIGHT HAVE TO TELL YOUR PRETTY LITTLE WIFE...

THEN TO SHUT YOU UP I'LL HAVE TO TAKE YOU OUT SOMETIME.
ALL RIGHT. ♡
IT'S A DEAL...
HA HA HA!
SEE YOU LATER!
blah
blah
......
DON'T YOU GOTTA MAKE UP SOME SORT OF EXCUSE?
OH, DON'T WORRY ABOUT IT.
HE WAS JUST KIDDING.
IF I MADE SOME LAME EXCUSE, IT'D LOOK MORE SUSPICIOUS.
YEAH, RIGHT.
OR IS THERE REALLY SOMETHING ELSE GOING ON?
HE WAS SO SMOOTH DEALING WITH THAT GUY.
MAYBE HE CHEATS ALL THE TIME?
SO THAT IS YOUR REAL NAME.
WELL, THAT'S GOOD. ♡
HUH?
OH, JUST THINKING OUT LOUD.
WELL, I GUESS I SHOULD GO THEN.

SO NO MORE CHEAT-ING!!
GULP
I'LL TRY NOT TO.
GOOD.
LIKE I SHOULD CARE.
AH HA HA
GOOD-BYE...
TAKASHI.
I REALLY DID...
LOVE YOU.
blah
blah

IT'S ALL RIGHT.
AIN'T GOT NO MORE TEARS LEFT TO CRY.
RING RING RING GNIRG
HUH? WHAT A STUPID RING TONE.
GOTTA CHANGE THAT.
HELLO, THIS IS NANA! ♡
HEY, YOU'RE ALL RIGHT.
KYOSUKE?
YOU SOUND GOOD-- HE MUST'VE FOUND YOU?
HUH?
WH-- WHO?
OH, WELL, I DIDN'T THINK HE WOULD.
I JUST HOPED IT'D ALL WORK OUT.
WHERE ARE YOU NOW?

I'M NEAR THE HOTEL. I'M ALMOST THERE.
YOU FREAKED ME OUT, I THOUGHT YOU MEANT TAKASHI...
WELL, ABOUT AN HOUR AGO, SHOJI AND JUNKO FREAKED OUT AND WENT LOOKING FOR YOU.
I KNEW IF THEY FOUND YOU, IT'D BE CRAZY, LIKE TV DRAMA...
YOU LOVE IT, DON'T YOU, PLAYING MY FEELINGS BY GETTING ALL TEARY-EYED AND SAYING THINGS TO GET ME STOKED?
I'M SORRY, I...
I DIDN'T MEAN TO...
YOU DON'T HAVE TO APOLOGIZE TO ME...
BUT I...
SNIFF
OR CRY TO ME EITHER.
BUT ...
SOB
IT'S ALL RIGHT.
SHOJI'S JUST IN LOVE WITH YOU.
YEAH, RIGHT!
I AM RIGHT!
AND YOU KNOW IT.

KYOSUKE ...
I WONDER WHERE SHOJI IS NOW...
BUT FOR NOW, YOU SHOULD JUST GET BACK TO THE HOTEL...
CLICK
....
beep beep beep
WHO KNOWS?
BUT HE'S PROBABLY NOT FAR...
DING DONG
KYOSUKE! I CAN'T FIND HER!
IT'D BE BETTER TO JUST CALL HER CELL PHONE INSTEAD OF LOOKING FOR HER!
SO YOU FINALLY FIGURED THAT OUT.
ACTU-ALLY, I'VE ALWAYS LOVED HIM.

FROM THE MOMENT I FIRST LAID EYES ON HIM...
I THOUGHT HE WAS SO FINE.
BUT I WAS STILL RECOVERING THEN.
MAYBE IT WAS MASOCHISTIC, BUT I WAS SO HURT.
I WAS SCARED OF SPREADING MY PAIN.
I COULDN'T HAVE A GOOD RELATIONSHIP.
I COULDN'T TRUST MEN.
BUT SHOJI SEEMED DIFFERENT.
MAYBE NOT REALLY DIFFERENT, BUT HE WAS DIFFERENT TO ME.

WHENEVER I WAS WITH YOU, IT FELT LIKE I WAS BEING HEALED.
YOU ALWAYS WRAPPED ME GENTLY IN YOUR HEART.
RIGHT NOW, WITH THAT WARMTH...
I WANT YOU TO HOLD ME TIGHT.
NANA !!

PLEASE...
HOLD ME.
blah
blah
blah
bla
HA!
WHAT'S WITH THE FACE?
HA?
UM...
I'M SORRY ABOUT EARLI-ER.
I WENT TOO FAR.
LET'S JUST NOT WORRY ABOUT IT.
....

THIS ISN'T WORKING!!
BEEP
MAYBE IT'S JUST TOO LATE...
...FOR US TO DATE NOW.
WHRRRR
......
SEVENTH FLOOR.
SEVEN...
IT'S BAD LUCK!!
WELCOME BACK. ♡
JUN, MAN, DO YOU KNOW WHAT SHOJI DID?!
GOOD NIGHT.
CLICK

707
ROOM 707 ...
OH PLEASE, NO...
WHY ARE YOU TALKING TO YOURSELF?
YOU'RE SCARING ME.
I WASN'T TALKING TO MYSELF! I WAS TALKING TO THE DEMON LORD.
THAT'S EVEN SCARIER!
PLOP
OH—MAN— I'M EXHAUSTED FROM RUNNING AROUND.
TALK ABOUT BEING A PAIN IN THE ASS...
LOOK WHO'S TALKING— YOU'RE THE ONE WHO DITCHED ME!

MAN...
WHY ARE WE BEING SO MEAN TO EACH OTHER...
I SHOULD BE NICE TO THE GUY I LIKE.
I HATE THIS.
I GUESS IT'S NO USE ANYMORE.
I PUSHED SHOJI TOO FAR AWAY.
HE'S NOT EVEN NERVOUS ANY-MORE WHEN WE'RE IN THE SAME ROOM.
HE JUST SEEMS BORED.
HEY, NANA...
I REALLY WANT TO MOVE TO TOKYO AND TAKE YOU WITH ME.
BUT, YA KNOW, I HAVEN'T GOT MY LIFE TO-GETHER YET.
MAYBE IF I WAS A COLLEGE STUDENT, BUT I'M NOT IN YET.
AND EVEN IF YOU WERE HOMELESS AND DYING, THERE WOULDN'T BE MUCH I COULD DO.
AS A "MAN", THAT'S HARD FOR ME.
PLEASE UNDER-STAND.

THEN ...
THEN I'LL STAY HOME ...
WORK, AND SAVE UP MONEY TO MOVE TO TOKYO!
...
THEN NEXT YEAR, IF YOU GET INTO COLLEGE, I'LL GO TO TOKYO, TOO!
AND AFTER I MOVE, I'LL TRY TO FIND A JOB THAT PAYS ENOUGH TO LIVE ON MY OWN!
WON'T THAT BE COOL ?
...
THEN I GUESS I BETTER GET INTO COL-LEGE.
WATCH OUT DEMON LORD!

AW-RIGHT!
NOW THAT WE'VE MADE UP...
I GUESS WE CAN FINALLY DO IT!
WHAT?
I GUESS...
LIKE IT'S SOME GOAL...
WE HAVEN'T EVEN SMOOCHED YET!
IT'S ALL RIGHT.
DON'T JUST SHUT DOWN ON ME!
IF YOU DON'T WANNA, WE DON'T HAVE TO.
I'M USED TO HOLDING BACK.
......
DOESN'T HE KNOW ABOUT GETTING IN THE MOOD?
ALL RIGHT THEN...
WHAT DO YOU WANNA SAY ABOUT IT?
HUH?
UM...
MAYBE IF YOU COULD EVEN SAY "I LOVE YOU," I'D DO IT.
"LOVE"?

AS IF THAT WORD MEANS ANYTHING.
AND YOU CAN'T MAKE A GUY SAY IT!
BUT NO ONE HAS EVER SAID IT TO ME SINCE THE DAY I WAS BORN.
I'D LIKE TO HEAR IT AT LEAST ONCE BEFORE I DIE.
BUT WHAT DOES IT MEAN IF YOU HAVE TO ASK FIRST?
GOD, JUST FORGET IT.
SHOVE
....
ALL RIGHT, I GET IT.
BUT I'M A DUDE. I'LL SAY IT.
I'LL JUST HAVE TO PRETEND I'M SOMEONE ELSE...
WHAT?!
LIKE A SENSITIVE GUY.
POP
AM I SUPPOSED TO PRETEND I'M DOING IT WITH SOMEONE ELSE?
I DON'T WANNA, UNLESS IT'S YOU, WEIRDO.
I'M GONNA MAKE SOME TEA.
WHADDYA WANT, SENSITIVE GUY, GREEN OR ROASTED TEA?
Slap

NANA ...?
SHOJI ...
I HEARD IT...
YOUR HEART ....
...TOLD ME YOU LOVED ME.
I GUESS YOU HEARD IT THEN...

I WANTED TO HAVE A GOOD RELATIONSHIP.
ONE THAT'S ROMANTIC AND DRAMATIC, LIKE IN THE MOVIES.
BUT I FINALLY BECAME A WOMAN AT 17...
AND LEARNED THAT MEN AREN'T REALLY THAT SIMPLE.
OR SO I THOUGHT.

THAT NIGHT HELD THE SWEET TASTE OF HAPPI-NESS...
AND MY BODY FELT LIKE IT WAS GONNA MELT.
I HOPE EVERY-THING WORKED OUT WITH THOSE TWO.
I'M WOR-RIED.

WELL, THEY SHOULDN'T NEED MY HELP TO GET TOGETHER.
IT'S NOT LIKE THEY'RE IN JUNIOR HIGH.
......
HEY!
SNORE
DON'T MAKE ME SIT HERE AND TALK TO MYSELF.
Whip
I'M GOING TO BED.
A WOMAN'S LIFE ISN'T SOME-THING TO SNEER AT, IS IT JUN? ♡
ZZZ ZZZ
FLIP
ZZZ ZZZ

BUT IT'S A LONG-DISTANCE RELATIONSHIP...
WHAT?
OH, NOTHING.
VIDEO RENTAL
THAT'LL BE ¥300 IN LATE FEES, SIR.
OH...
ALL RIGHT.
貸出カウンター
WHAT'S YOUR PROBLEM? I'M NOT THE ONE LATE RETURNING GROSS PORN!
MEN!
THEY'RE ALL SO LAME.
HEY, NANA...
WANNA GO HAVE DINNER WITH ME TONIGHT?
MR. NAKAMURA...
THAT'S KINDA INAPPROPRIATE.

TOO LATE FOR YOU DUDE, 22-YEAR-OLD NAKAMURA.
HE'S YOUNGER THAN I THOUGHT...
OH COME ON, IT'S ONLY DINNER.
...AND SO LOOSE.
AREN'T YOU LONELY WITH YOUR BOY-FRIEND OFF IN TOKYO?
...AND PERSIS-TENT.
YOU USED TO LIKE ME.
YEAH, WHAT-EVER.
UGH...
MAYBE I SHOULD QUIT WORKING THERE.
BUT THE PAY IS GOOD.
YOU SHOULD QUIT, NAKAMURA.
AND I GOTTA HURRY UP AND SAVE MORE TO MOVE TO TOKYO.
I CAN'T WAIT 'TIL SPRING.
♫ RING RING
HI, THIS IS NANA! ♡
OH, HI...
SHOJI?
YEAH!
I'M GREAT, MAN!

NANA KOMATSU.
NINETEEN YEARS OLD.
IN A RELATIONSHIP, BUT LONG-DISTANCE.
JUST YOU WAIT AND SEE, DEMON LORD!

I HAVE NO IDEA WHERE I WAS BORN.

I'VE NEVER SEEN MY FATHER'S FACE...

AND I'VE LONG FORGOTTEN
THE FACE OF MY MOTHER.

I CAME TO THIS COASTAL VILLAGE
WHEN I WAS FOUR YEARS OLD.

I WAS RAISED BY MY GRANDMOTHER,
WHO RAN A SMALL DINER
AND CONSTANTLY DUMPED HER
COLD SARCASM ON ME.

THESE DAYS, WHILE WORKING TIRELESSLY...

I POLISH THE SHARDS OF MY DREAMS.

NANA

ナナ

LA-DIES AND GERMS ...
WE'RE BLAST!
TONIGHT 7:00~
TODAY'S MENU
★Nonsensical
★Scrape
★WONDERWALL
★Blast Black Stones
CLUB Z

REN
NANA
HEY!
THEY'RE COMING OUT NOW!
Oooh!

NANA
REN
YASU
NOBU
NO WAY!
IT'S PISS COLD, AND YOU ALL JUST WAITED HERE FOR US?
WOW! THANKS, MAN!
NANA! YOU GUYS WERE AWE-SOME!
EEK EEK
SO~~ CUTE~~
OH, THANK YOU! ♡
YEAH, YOU COME TO EVERY SHOW!
AND YOU'RE CUTE. ♡
NANA, IT WAS YOUR BIRTHDAY LAST WEEK, RIGHT?
NANA!
SHOVE
HERE'S A PRES-ENT FOR YOU!
HEY, WHAT'S THIS? VIVIENNE WEST-WOOD?!
MISATO, ARE YOU SURE?
THIS IS SUPER EXPEN-SIVE.
YOU...
YOU REMEM-BERED MY NAME?
SO IT'S YOUR BIRTHDAY PRESENT. HAPPY 18TH!
WOW, YOU KNEW?

SMOOCH
THANK YOU.
Shreeek
COOL, I GOT ME SOME VIVI-ENNE.
ALL RIGHT!
HERE'S TO A GREAT SHOW TONIGHT, GUYS.
居酒屋
WELL– I GOTTA SAY WE KICKED ASS AT TONIGHT'S BATTLE OF THE BANDS.

I BET MOST OF THE PEOPLE THERE TONIGHT WERE OUR FANS.
TO THINK THE DAY WOULD COME IN MY LIFE WHEN GIRLS WOULD LIKE ME! ♡
HAPPINESS ♡
BUT THEY ALL DRESS UP LIKE NANA... PRETTY SCARY.
THAT EYELINER.
WHOA!
IT'S A JACKET! THAT'S SO COOL!
LIMITED EDITION. I WONDER HOW MUCH THIS COST?
I BET THAT GIRL IS GETTIN' PUMMELED BY THE OTHER FANS RIGHT NOW.
I FEEL BAD FOR HER.
I GUESS MY KISS'LL COST HER IN MORE WAYS THAN ONE.
HEH HEH! ♡
PURE EVIL.
HEY!
HEY MISS, REFILL?
SUPER-SIZE ME!
NOBU... YOU BETTER STOP.
ISN'T GRADUATION TOMORROW?
ARE YOU GOING TO HIS GRADUATION, NANA?
EXCUSE ME FOR BEING A HIGH SCHOOL DROP-OUT!
SO WHAT? I ONLY GRADUATED FROM JUNIOR HIGH!
DON'T BRAG!
AH HA HA!
HEY, THE LAW STUDENT'S LAUGHING.
WHAT A SARCASTIC BASTARD.
MAN, I WISH I COULDA SEEN NANA IN A SCHOOL UNIFORM.
DID SHE WEAR BAGGY SOCKS?
YOU REALLY WOULDN'T WANNA SEE IT, YASU.
SHE WAS SERIOUSLY SCARY.
I WAS SO SCARED I WOULDN'T EVEN TALK TO HER.
YOU LIAR.
YOU TOTALLY STALKED ME.
YOU WERE SO OBNOXIOUS.
YEAH, RIGHT.
I DID IT 'CAUSE YOU LOOKED SO LONELY ALL THE TIME.
I CAN SEE IT NOW... NOBU STALKING NANA.
HEH HEH
I WAS YOUR ONLY FRIEND.
SHOW ME SOME LOVE!

Let's hear it for BLaaaaaast-t-t-t-t!
....
THUD
crash crash
HE'S TOTALLY OUT.
JUST LEAVE HIM. LET'S GO HOME.
WHAT IF HE DIES?
GIGGLE
I'M SURE HE WILL.
SERIOUSLY
WHO DO YA THINK I AM? I'LL NEVER GET CAUGHT!
HEY!
I'LL ELUDE THEM ALL!
...
DID YOU DO SOMETHING?
REN, WAIT!
I'LL LUG HIM HOME IN A CAB.
OF COURSE YASU WOULD, THE RICH MAN. ♡
WHAT ELSE WOULD YOU EXPECT FROM A LAW SCHOOL GUY!
WILL YOU MARRY ME? ♡
YASU ...
WHEN NANA GETS THROWN IN THE SLAMMER, WILL YOU BE HER LAWYER?

ABOUT THAT THING...
I'LL TALK TO NOBU.
MAKE SURE AND TELL NANA.
WHAT?
THAT THING...
WELL, THE REASON YASU'S A SKINHEAD IS 'CAUSE HE STARTED TO GROW A LITTLE BALD SPOT.
THOSE WHO LAUGH AT BALDY WILL CRY WHEN THEY GO BALD!
WOW, PLAYING LIVE IS IT FOR ME, MAN.
HOW CAN I SAY IT?
OR-GAS-MIC?
OOOH-- IT FELT SO GOOD IT WAS DANGER-OUS!
HA HA!
THAT'S COOL, MAN.
YEAH. IT WAS SO RAD. ♡
I FEEL... SO~~~ GREAT~~~
BETTER THAN DOING IT WITH A GUY?
I GUESS THAT DEPENDS ON THE GUY. ♡

Whoosh
OH-HH...
IT'S FREEZ-ING!!
I'M GONNA GET SICK!
WHAT IF I LOSE MY BEAU-TIFUL SINGING VOICE?!
IS THERE AN INSTANT HAND WARMER IN HERE?
MAN, INCON-SIDERATE FANS.
WE TRY TO LOOK COOL, BUT WE'RE HOT IN THE SUMMER AND COLD IN THE WINTER!
THERE'S GOTTA BE SOME-THING...
SOME-THING WE CAN WRAP AROUND US.
GOT IT.
REN

COOL
!!

REN • NANA
REN HONJO
NANA OSAKI
HEY, REN ...
'MEMBER WHEN ...
...WE FIRST MET?
IT WAS A BLIZZARD JUST LIKE THIS.
YEAH, I REMEMBER.
... REALLY ?
YEAH, AT THE CHRISTMAS SHOW, A COUPLE YEARS AGO.
TWO YEARS AND THREE MONTHS AGO.
YEAH, WHEN I WAS PLAYING GUITAR FOR THAT OTHER BAND...
WITH GIRLS FALLING ALL OVER ME...I WAS TOTALLY FULL OF MYSELF... JUST SCREWING AROUND, YA KNOW.
....
YEAH, WHATEVER.

YOU WERE WEARING A RED DRESS THAT NIGHT.
GO ON ...
HUMPH
YOU WERE STANDING FRONT AND CENTER, JUST GLARING AT ME, STIFF AS A CORPSE.
I WAS SO PISSED, LIKE "WHAT'S HER PROBLEM?!"
....
stamp
... WAS I?
YOU EVEN REMEMBER WHAT I WORE ...
RAIN MAN.
I COULDN'T FORGET IT EVEN IF I WANTED TO.
YOU WERE THE MOST UNIMPRESSED AUDIENCE MEMBER EVER.
AND THEN NOBU DRAGGED YOU BACKSTAGE AFTERWARDS.
YOU WERE SO HARSH.
NO SMILE.
"I'M NANA."
THAT'S IT.
YOU JUST COULDN'T BE NICE...
IF IT KILLED YOU.
I HAD A LOT GOING ON THEN. I WAS JUST BEING ANTI-SOCIAL.
SURE.
'CAUSE YOU GOT CAUGHT TURNING TRICKS AND GOT EXPELLED!
DID NOT! I WAS FALSELY ACCUSED!
YOU'RE THE DUDE WHO STOLE MY VIRGINITY!
... WELL, EXCUUUSE ME!
DOWN, GIRL.

Y'KNOW, I'M SURPRISED YOU TOOK IT SO QUIETLY CONSIDERING HOW HOT-HEADED YOU ARE.
I DIDN'T EVEN HAVE THE ENERGY TO FREAK OUT BACK THEN.
... YEAH ...
YOU LOOKED BEATEN UP.
BODY SOAP
I THOUGHT IT WAS MY ONLY CHANCE, 'CAUSE I WAS THINKING ABOUT QUITTING SCHOOL SO I COULD WORK.
BUT WEREN'T YOU BEING USED LIKE A SERVANT BY YOUR MEAN OLD GRANDMOTHER?
WHY WOULD YOU WANNA WORK ANY MORE THAN THAT?
I NEEDED MONEY.
.....
MY GRANDMA NEVER GAVE ME A CENT.
AH HA HA!
IT'S NOT FUNNY!!
I KNOW, I KNOW.
SORRY.
SCRUB SCRUB
EVER SINCE I WAS A KID, YA KNOW?
EVERYONE ELSE HAD MONEY FROM THEIR 'RENTS TO DO WHATEVER THEY WANTED.
I THOUGHT, "WHY AM I THE ONLY KID WITH NOTHING?"
BUT YOU'RE NOT A KID ANYMORE, SO YOUR LIFE NOW IS WHAT YOU MAKE OF IT.

AND IT WASN'T UNTIL RECENTLY THAT I REALIZED HOW LUCKY I WAS TO EVEN HAVE MY GRANDMA.
IT IS, ISN'T IT?
YEAH, SHE WAS A MEAN OLD LADY, BUT...
AT HER AGE, A SINGLE WOMAN RUNNING A SHOP AND RAISING A KID, IT MUST'VE BEEN REALLY HARD.
NO WONDER SHE WAS SO NASTY.
I NEVER GOT TO TELL HER I APPRECIATED HER BEFORE SHE DIED.
IT WAS LIKE I'D KILLED HER.
DID YOU PUSH HER DOWN A FLIGHT OF STAIRS?
THEN I'D REALLY BE A KILLER!
BUT THERE WERE TIMES I GOT SO PISSED OFF AT HER I WANTED TO PUSH HER.
......
GOOD THING YOU DIDN'T.
BUT I DID SOMETHING WORSE.
LIKE WHAT ...?
SHE DIED OF SHOCK WHEN I GOT KICKED OUTTA HIGH SCHOOL.
HOW BAD COULD IT BE? ....
SHE GOT INCREDIBLY DEPRESSED WHEN I DIDN'T DENY THE PROSTITUTION CHARGE.
....
SHE BECAME BEDRIDDEN, AND IN LESS THAN A MONTH, SHE GOT SICK AND DIED.

I THINK SHE LOST THE WILL TO LIVE.
I SHOULD'VE DENIED THE CHARGES, FOR HER...
I KNOW I TOLD YOU ABOUT IT BEFORE.
MY MOTHER...
...WHEN I WAS FOUR YEARS OLD, SHE SENT ME TO GRANDMA'S AND JUST DISAPPEARED.
LIKE A PROVERB, GRANDMA WOULD ALWAYS TELL ME...
...THAT MY MOTHER HAD ME WITHOUT EVER KNOWING WHO MY FATHER WAS.
THAT SHE WAS THE TYPE OF GIRL WHO'D RUN OFF WITH A GUY 'CAUSE I GOT IN THE WAY.
AND THAT I SHOULD NEVER GROW UP TO BE LIKE HER.
THAT'S WHY SHE NEVER LET ME WEAR PINK OR RED.
SHE SAID IF I DRESSED LIKE THAT, IT MEANT I WAS SEDUCING MEN. ♡

AH HA HA!
LAUGH ALL YOU WANT!
BUT WHEN YOU'RE RAISED LIKE THAT, YOU GET BRAINWASHED INTO BELIEVING IT.
RAISING A CHILD IS A KIND OF BRAINWASHING.
TERROR
BUT I WAS A GIRL, YA KNOW?
I WANTED TO WEAR CUTESY CLOTHES.
YOU WANT IT MORE WHEN YOU CAN'T HAVE IT.

SO AFTER LOSING GRANDMA, I WAS ALL ALONE.
I DECIDED TO BUY POOR OLD ME A CHRISTMAS PRESENT WITH MONEY I'D SAVED FROM WORK.
SO OF COURSE, I BOUGHT A BRIGHT RED FRILLY DRESS.
I REMEMBER WEARING IT TO THE SHOW THAT NIGHT... I WAS SO PSYCHED...
'CAUSE NOBU SAID HE'D INTRODUCE ME TO SOME SUPER COOL DUDE.
YEAH, RIGHT.
YOU JUST TOLD ME YOU WERE TOTALLY PISSED OFF.
THAT'S BECAUSE THERE WAS SUCH AN AMAZING LADY STAND-ING RIGHT IN FRONT OF ME.
AND IT LOOKED LIKE I DIDN'T HAVE A CHANCE.
SO YOUR GRANDMA WAS RIGHT!
YOU SEDUCED ME WITH THAT FRILLY RED DRESS!
WHAT-EVER ...

I HID THAT RED DRESS ...
UNDER MY COAT.
AND RAN THROUGH THE BLIZ-ZARD.
LIVE HOUSE
HE WAS AHEAD OF ME IN JUNIOR HIGH.
HE'S TWO YEARS OLDER.
HE'S TOTALLY COOL.
YOU'RE GONNA LOVE HIM.
I'LL INTRODUCE HIM TO YOU LATER.
OH DON'T WORRY ABOUT IT.
I'M JUST GOING FOR THE SHOW.
I'M TELLING YOU, MAN, A PROBLEM CHILD LIKE YOU...
NEEDS AN OPEN-MINDED GUY.
REN'S A GREAT GUY, AS LONG AS YOU CAN IGNORE HIS WOMANIZING AND THE GIRLS HANGING ALL OVER HIM.
I DON'T NEED THAT KIND OF GUY.

YOU'D LIKE HIM IF YOU JUST MET HIM AND TALKED TO HIM.
HE'S A LOT MORE TOGETHER THAN MOST PEOPLE WE KNOW.
HE GREW UP IN FOSTER CARE, SO I THINK HE PROBABLY ALSO HAD A HARD LIFE.
......
ACTUALLY...
I GUESS REN WAS ABANDONED IN THE HARBOR WAREHOUSE DISTRICT RIGHT AFTER HE WAS BORN.
IT WAS EVEN ON THE NEWS.
NOBUO...
YOU SHOULDN'T GOSSIP ABOUT PEOPLE'S PERSONAL STUFF LIKE THAT.
NO, IT'S COOL.
REN ALWAYS BRAGS ABOUT IT.
HE BRAGS ABOUT IT?
HE'S ALWAYS BRAGGING THAT THERE AREN'T MANY PEOPLE WHO CAN SAY THEY'VE BEEN IN THE NEWS SINCE THE DAY THEY WERE BORN.
AND TO TOP IT OFF, REN'S LIVING IN THAT SAME WAREHOUSE DISTRICT TODAY.
HE CLAIMS IT AS HIS BIRTHPLACE.
......
REN WANTS TO BE A BIG ROCK STAR.
HE SAYS HIS SCANDALOUS PERSONAL HISTORY GIVES HIM SEX APPEAL!
GIMME A BREAK, THAT'S STUPID.
WHAT?!
IT'S SO COOL, MAN!
HE'S MARKETING HIS PERSONAL MISFORTUNE AND TRYING TO BUY PITY.
HOW LAME.

BUT THE GUY UP ON STAGE ...
NAILED ME TO THE FLOOR.

SO THIS IS THE GUY THEY SAY WAS ABANDONED IN THE HARBOR WAREHOUSE DISTRICT...
...THE STORY HE BRAGS ABOUT.

WHAT CAME OVER ME THAT NIGHT...
I DON'T KNOW HOW TO SAY IT.
IT WASN'T SO SIMPLE ...
AS "LOVE" OR "DESIRE."
MORE LIKE JEAL-OUSY, ENVY ...
A SENSE OF UNEAS-INESS ...
AND NEED.

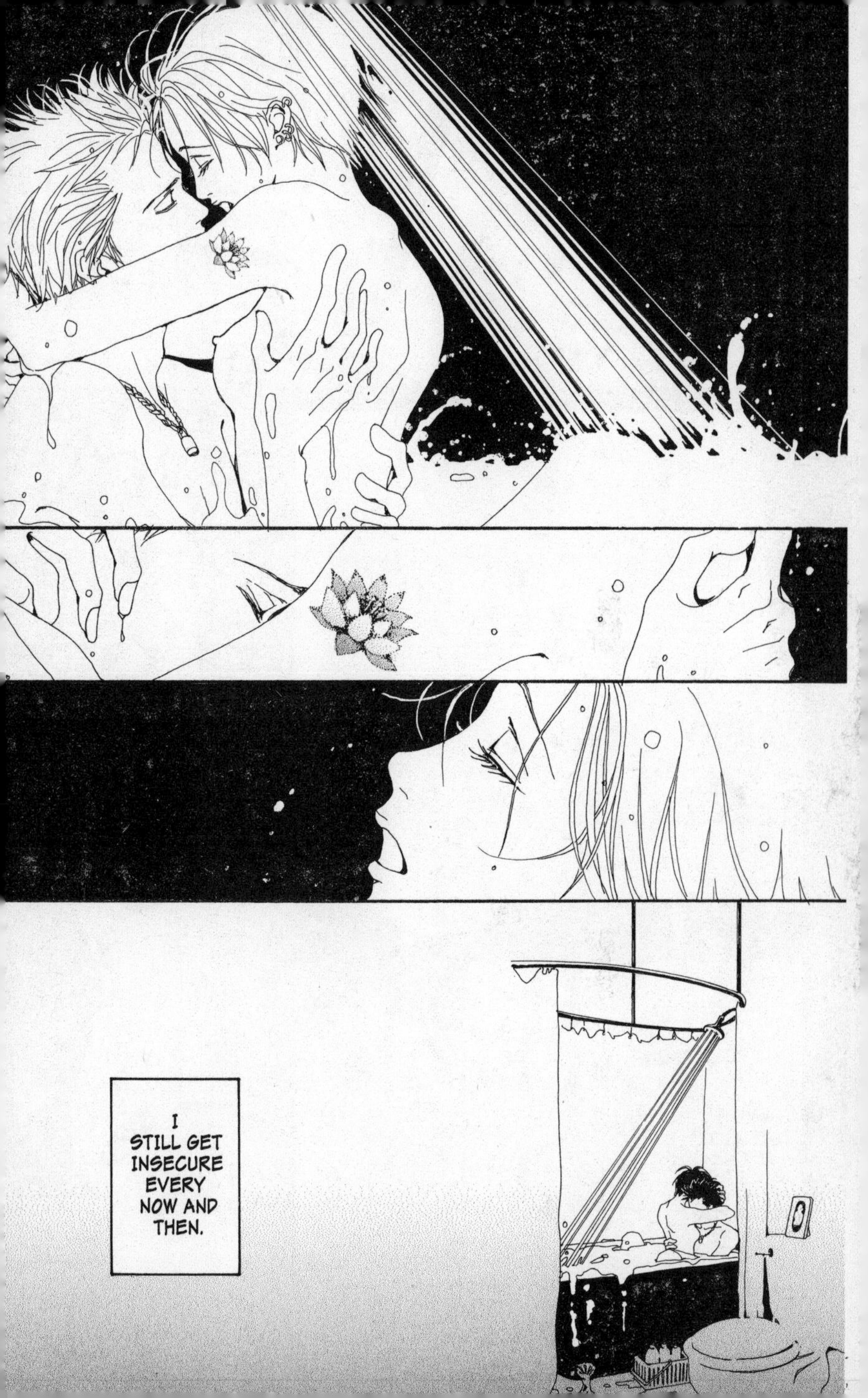
I STILL GET INSECURE EVERY NOW AND THEN.

SID & NANCY
LOVE KILLS
BECAUSE IT FEELS LIKE EVERY DAY WITH REN...
...IS JUST A DREAM.
REN WAS TOO GLAMOROUS FOR THE MUNDANE LIFE I'D BEEN LIVING UP 'TIL THEN.
NO MATTER HOW I'VE STRUGGLED, I COME UP LACKING, STILL.
I WISH WE COULD DO IT IN A BIGGER PLACE.
YEAH, THAT BATHTUB'S TOO SMALL.
I MEAN PLAYING A SHOW!
WE'VE GOT A LOT OF FANS NOW. I THINK WE SHOULD TRY TO PLAY A BIGGER PLACE.

WHY DON'T YOU MAKE IT HAPPEN ?
......
DON'T ACT LIKE IT'S JUST ON ME...
WHAT WAS YASU TALKING ABOUT WHEN WE WERE ALL GOING HOME?
SO ANY-WAYS ...
HE SOUNDED SERI-OUS.
IS IT ABOUT THE BAND ?
A LITTLE BALD SPOT IS SERIOUS BUSI-NESS.
WHAT-EVER ...
I'LL JUST ASK YASU.
I GOTTA TAKE MY DRUGS ...
WHAT-EVER, JUNKIE.
AS IF! I'M TALKIN' ABOUT BIRTH CONTROL, YOU LOSER! IF I FORGET TO TAKE IT, WE'RE IN BIG TROUBLE. AND YOU KNOW IT!
WHAT WOULD WE DO IF I GOT PREG-NANT ?!
YOU'RE SUCH A BUM!
WE'D HAVE A BABY.
SINCE I DIDN'T GO TO HIGH SCHOOL, I WORKED HARD MANUAL LABOR JOBS, SO I'M ACTUALLY PRETTY FLUSH.
I'D BE TOTALLY FINE WITH ONE OR TWO KIDS.

WELL, EVEN IF YOU'RE FINE WITH IT, I'M NOT.
I WANNA PLAY MUSIC AND HAVE A LIFE.
NANA...

I'M GOING TO TOKYO.
SO YOU CAN HAVE WHATEVER LIFE YOU WANT.

TOKYO ...?
SO NOW WHAT?
WHAT ABOUT COLLEGE, YASU? ARE YOU GONNA DROP OUT?
WEREN'T YOU GONNA BE A LAWYER?
I DIDN'T SAY ME—REN.
ARE YOU LISTENING TO ME?
Splash
'MEMBER THAT ONE BAND?
WHEN REN AND I WERE IN OUR OTHER BAND, THERE WAS THIS BAND WE ALWAYS PLAYED AGAINST IN THE BATTLE OF THE BANDS?
TRAP-NEST.
TRAP...
OH YEAH, T-NEST!
THE BAND THAT HAD THAT RAD GIRL SINGER!
tap
WE USED TO BE DRINKING BUDDIES AND GOT PRETTY FRIENDLY.
ABOUT TWO YEARS AGO THEY ALL MOVED TO TOKYO TO TRY AND MAKE IT.
THEY JUST GOT SIGNED.
No way!
Unbelievable!

THEY WERE REALLY GOOD...
BUT I CAN'T BELIEVE IT!
WHEN THEY WERE ABOUT TO RE-LEASE THEIR RECORD, THEY HAD "IRRECONCILABLE DIFFERENCES" AND THE GUITARIST QUIT.
SO THE REST OF THEM DECIDED TO...
...ASK REN TO JOIN THEIR BAND.
REN LEFT THIS MORNING TO MEET WITH THEIR PRODUCER IN TOKYO.
BUT THEY ALREADY KNOW WHAT A GREAT AXE MAN HE IS.
SO IT'S REALLY JUST A FORMALITY. IT'S PRACTICALLY A DONE DEAL.

WHAT THE HELL ...?!
HE HASN'T MOVED TO TOKYO YET.
HE'LL BE COMING BACK FOR A BIT TOMORROW.
BUT HE *IS* MOVING TO TOKYO, ISN'T HE?
WHAT ABOUT BLAST?
WHAT ARE WE SUPPOSED TO DO?
WE'VE BEEN A BAND FOR ONLY A YEAR AND A HALF.
THINGS WERE JUST STARTING TO TAKE OFF. I CAN'T BELIEVE THIS...
NO BIG DEAL.
WE CAN FIND ANYONE TO PLAY BASS.
I'M SURE WE'LL FIND SOMEONE RIGHT AWAY.
BUT ...
I JUST DON'T GET IT.
WHY WOULD HE SCREW US LIKE THAT?
IT'D BE STUPID FOR REN TO JUST STAY IN THIS STALE OLD TOWN FOREVER, WASTING AWAY.

THEN LET'S FOLLOW REN TO TOKYO AND GO FOR IT, TOO!
BLAST OFF TOKYO!
I DON'T KNOW... I DON'T WANNA MAKE MUSIC BE MY WHOLE LIFE.
I DON'T WANNA GAM-BLE MY LIFE AWAY LIKE THAT.
BUT WHY?!
WHO SAYS WE'D GET SIGNED, TOO?
WELL, WE COULD TRY!
NO MATTER HOW HARD THEY TRY, A LOT OF BANDS JUST DON'T MAKE IT.
AND EVEN IF WE ALL MOVED TO TOKYO...
REN WILL HAVE TO MAKE T-NEST HIS PRIORITY.
I DON'T WANT THAT TO HAPPEN TO REN.
THIS IS HIS CHANCE.
NO MATTER WHAT, HE SHOULD GO FOR IT.
Blast
Cherry

BUT JUST 'CAUSE T-NEST GOT SIGNED DOESN'T MEAN THEY'LL "MAKE IT"...
MAYBE, BUT...
I THINK THEY'LL DO GOOD.
THEY HAVE THE RIGHT SOUND AND IMAGE.
ADD REN TO THE MIX AND THEY'VE GOT IT MADE.
BUT ?!
YOU JUST DON'T GET IT!
IF YOU WAN-NA GO TO TOKYO, JUST GO!
BUT DON'T STAND IN REN'S WAY!
BESIDES, YOU'RE GONNA IN-HERIT THE TERASHIMA INN, ANY-WAY.
THAT'S WHY YOU CAN RUN AROUND WITHOUT A JOB.
......
YOU CAN'T TRY TO MAKE IT IN MUSIC AND TAKE OVER THE FAMILY BUSINESS AT THE SAME TIME.
JUST DO THE BAND AS A SIDE PROJECT.
BUT ...
WHAT ABOUT NANA ...?
WILL REN...
JUST SPLIT ON NANA?

DON'T BE TALKIN' THAT SMACK.
HE HAS TO TAKE HER WITH!
WHAT THE HELL ...
"DON'T LEAVE HER!" "TAKE HER WITH!"
AS IF NANA'S JUST REN'S PET CAT OR SOME-THING.
YASU...
YOU'RE SO MATURE.
LEAVE IT TO THE DRUMMER, HE'S THE OLDEST.
?
......
SHE'S AN INDEPENDENT WOMAN, SUCCESSFUL IN HER OWN RIGHT.
IF SHE WANTS TO GO WITH HIM, SHE'LL GO.
THAT'S NANA'S CALL.
I'M SURE REN'S THOUGHT ABOUT IT.
JUST 'CAUSE YOU'RE SUCH A KID.
BUT IF NANA MOVES TO TOKYO WITH REN...
BLAST WILL HAVE TO BREAK UP.

IT'S UP TO YOU...

...NOBU, TO FIND NEW BAND MEMBERS.

HEY NOBU...
WANNA BE IN A BAND WITH US?

NOBUO'S ROOM, TERASHIMA INN
Splash
... HUH ...
WHAT ?
WHY ?
WHAT HAPPENED TO YOUR OTHER BAND ?
WE BROKE UP.
THEY SUCK.
THEY DON'T CARE ANY-MORE.
THEY DON'T EVEN COME TO PRACTICE, BUT STILL BITCH AND MOAN.
YOU PLAYED GUITAR FOR FUN IN JUNIOR HIGH, DIDN'T YOU?
REN TOLD ME YOU TOTALLY SHRED. YOU CAN'T QUIT NOW.
WHA?
I CAN PLAY BASS, SO YOU COULD PLAY GUITAR.
ALL RIGHT, MAN!

YEAH, BUT ...
CAN A GUY WHO SAT OUT FOR A YEAR AND A HALF STILL SHRED?
IT'S COOL, MAN! I STILL PLAY EVERY DAY AT HOME!
I CAN PLAY ALL YOUR SONGS, REN!
AND I HAVE MY OWN SONGS, TOO.
!
WELL, LET'S DO IT!
SO ...
WHAT ABOUT VOCALS? WHO'S GONNA SING?
click click
THAT'S THE PROBLEM.
IF POSSIBLE, I WANT A GIRL.
I'M SICK OF DRAMA DUDES.
I KNOW WHAT YOU MEAN.
IF SHE CAN SING, GREAT...
BUT IT'D BE COOL IF SHE WAS HOT, TOO.
NOBU! A GIRL! FIND US A GIRL SINGER!
A FOXY ONE!
....
GREAT... ALREADY THE GO-FER.
IF YOU WANT A GIRL, THERE'S ALWAYS TONS SWARMING AROUND YOU, REN.
STOP TALKING SMACK, DUDE.
YOU KNOW WHAT'D HAPPEN IF A GIRL I DID IT WITH WAS IN THE BAND?
IT'D BE THE SOURCE OF ALL EVIL.
IT'D RUIN EVERY-THING.
....
MAYBE IT'D WORK OUT WITH SOME REAL LOVE.

KNOCK KNOCK
HE SAID "LOVE."
HEH HEH
YOU LAUGH AT LOVE. LOVE WILL MAKE YOU CRY.
NOBUO, A FRIEND OF YOURS IS HERE.
NANA.
CAN SHE COME UP?
YEAH, SEND HER UP.
NANA?
IT'S A GIRL!
IS SHE HOT?
HUH?
BUT YOU MET HER BEFORE.
YEAH.
YOU KNOW, NANA.

THE SECOND TIME I SAW REN...
WAS IN THE MIDDLE OF SUMMER...
THE AFTER-NOON SEA BREEZE STUCK TO MY SKIN.

HUH?
HEY, NANA...
NOBU!
HEY, NOBUO... HERE'S THE CD I BORROWED, THANKS.
UH, YEAH.
WELL, I BETTER GET GOING.
HAVE YOU EVER GONE TO KARAOKE WITH HER BEFORE?
HUH?
KARAOKE?
CAN SHE SING?
WHA...?
YEAH... ACTUALLY.

ALL RIGHT THEN!

FROM THAT DAY ON, I WAS LIKE...

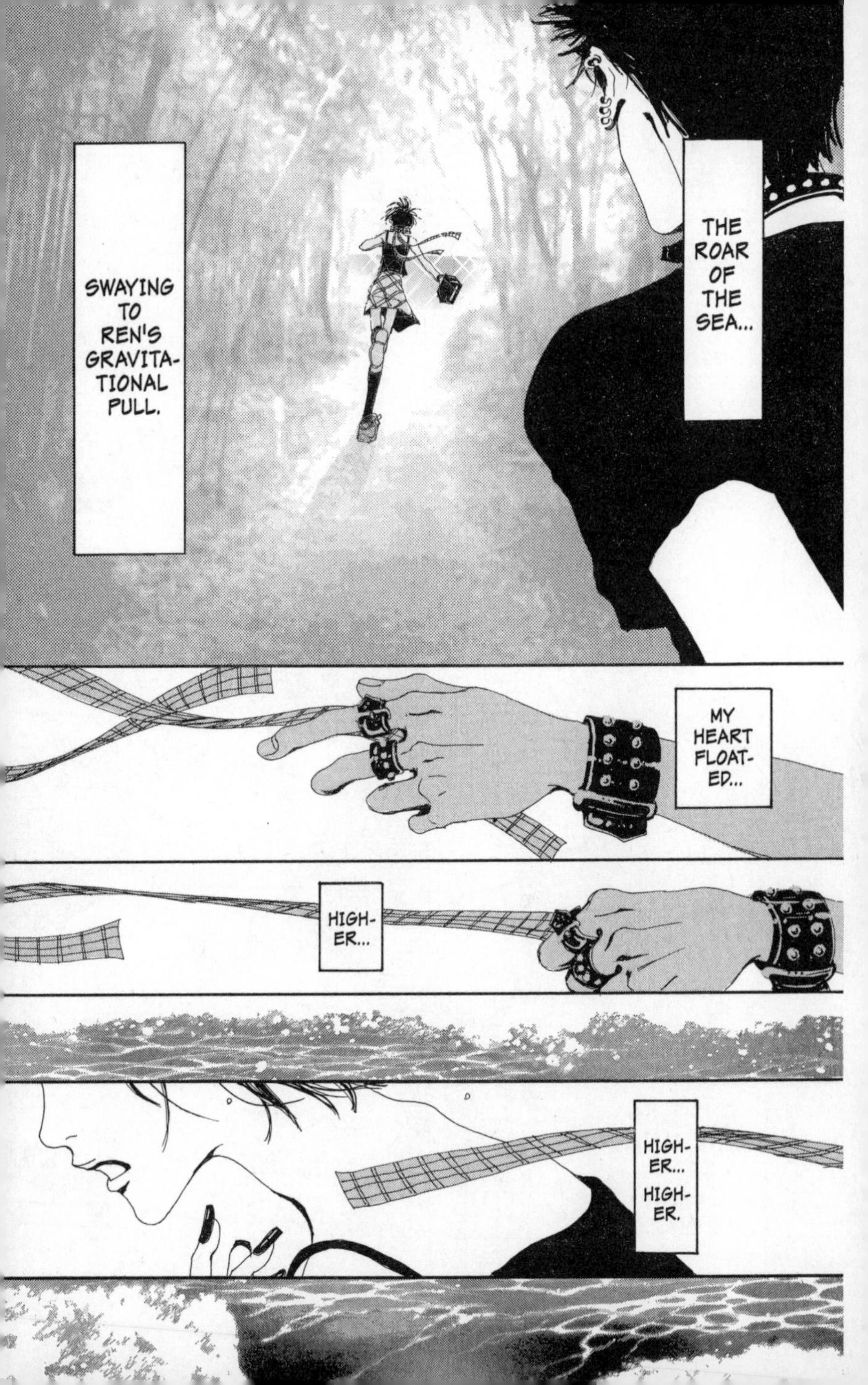
THE ROAR OF THE SEA...
SWAYING TO REN'S GRAVITATIONAL PULL.
MY HEART FLOATED...
HIGHER...
HIGHER... HIGHER.

HEY, NANA!
I WANT YOU TO SING IN THE BAND!
AND THIS GAVE VOICE TO MY INNER DESIRES.

BUT I WASN'T SINGING ...
FOR REN.
I SING EVERY DAY...
FOR MY-SELF.
BOOKS
ART SPACE
BONK

HEY LOOK!
Certificate of Graduation
NOBUO TERASHIMA
JEALOUS MUCH?
CHECK IT OUT...
NO BUTTONS LEFT ON MY UNIFORM.
WHAT ELSE CAN YOU EXPECT FROM BLAST'S GUITARIST?!
HOW MUCH DO YOU THINK MY SECOND BUTTON SOLD FOR?
YOU TOOK GIRLS' MONEY?!
BEAT IT SHRIMP, I'M BUSY.
YEAH RIGHT, THE STORE'S EMPTY.
HOW ARE YOU BUSY?
I'M BUSY READING!
YOU SHOULD TRY READING A BOOK INSTEAD OF JUST MANGA!
NOT THAT THERE'S ANYTHING WRONG WITH MANGA...
Season of Battle
SO, I HEARD ABOUT REN.
WHATCHA GONNA DO?
YOU GONNA MOVE TO TOKYO WITH HIM?
AW, YOU'RE HERE TO TRY AND STOP ME. WILL YOU MISS ME?
SNICKER.
FINE, GO TO TOKYO, AND I'LL GO, TOO!

WHAT ARE YOU TALKING ABOUT ...?
LET'S MOVE THE BAND TO TOKYO.
DON'T YOU WANNA SEE HOW FAR WE CAN GO WITH IT?
I'M NOT SAYING IT'LL BE EASY, BUT...
I THINK WE SHOULD AT LEAST TRY.
I THINK WITH YOUR VOICE WE CAN MAKE IT, NANA.
YOU'RE NOT PATSY CLINE OR ANY-THING...
BUT YOUR VOICE IS HUSKY AND COOL... UNIQUE.
I WANNA GO FOR IT.
I DON'T WANNA PLAY GUITAR WITH ANY OTHER SINGER...

YASU THINKS SO, TOO.
HE SAID HE'LL QUIT FOR GOOD IF YOU LEAVE.
DON'T SAY THAT...
WHY NOT?
'CAUSE THAT'S WHAT I WANTED TO HEAR FROM REN...
NOT JUST FROM YOU.
THANK YOU, NOBU...
BUT I'M NOT MOVING...
OPEN

BUT WHY NOT?
ARE YOU SPLIT-TING UP WITH REN?
EVEN IF YOU'RE NOT IN A BAND TOGETHER, YOU CAN STILL LIVE TOGETHER.
I CAN'T DO THAT!
NANA ...
IT'S ALL RIGHT.
REN WON'T THINK YOU'RE IN THE WAY IF YOU MOVE WITH HIM.
THAT PLAYER DIDN'T CHEAT ON YOU ONCE.
THAT'S PROOF HE'S IN LOVE WITH YOU.
I KNOW THAT...
..... OF COURSE YOU KNOW...
HE'S YOUR BOY-FRIEND.
MY LIFE DOESN'T REVOLVE AROUND SCREWING REN!
.....
I KNOW, BUT...
I WANNA BE A REAL SINGER.

THEN LET'S MOVE TO TOKYO!
I DON'T WANNA RIGHT NOW.
WHY NOT?
MAN, I DON'T GET YOU.
IF I MOVE NOW, I'LL JUST END UP LIVING WITH REN. I COULDN'T NOT LIVE WITH HIM.
I LOVE HIM.
SO LIVE WITH HIM.
I'D JUST BE WAITING AROUND AT HOME, WITH NO BAND OF MY OWN, MAKING MISO SOUP, WHILE REN GETS FAMOUS IN A BAND WITH A BETTER GIRL SINGER.
I AIN'T DOIN' THAT.
I GOT PRIDE ...

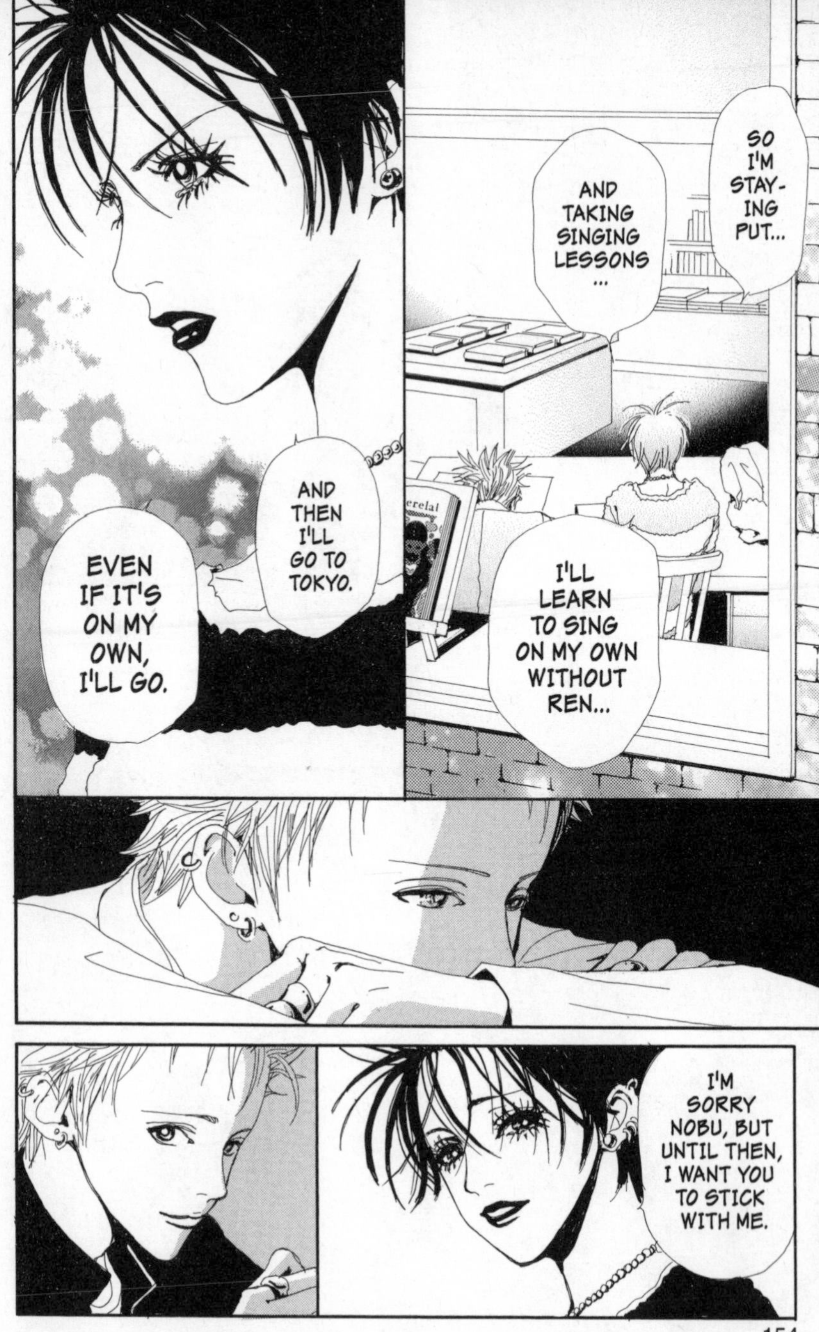
SO I'M STAYING PUT...
AND TAKING SINGING LESSONS...
I'LL LEARN TO SING ON MY OWN WITHOUT REN...
AND THEN I'LL GO TO TOKYO.
EVEN IF IT'S ON MY OWN, I'LL GO.
I'M SORRY NOBU, BUT UNTIL THEN, I WANT YOU TO STICK WITH ME.

YOU REALLY DON'T WANNA SING WITH-OUT ME PLAYING GUITAR?
NOT REALLY, WHY?

REN AND I HOOKED UP...
ABOUT A YEAR AFTER WE FIRST MET.

IT WAS CHRIST-MAS NIGHT.

MY ATTRAC-TION TO HIM NEVER WENT AWAY.
SO ONE NIGHT AFTER PLAYING A SHOW ...
WE SCREWED AROUND TOGETHER...
ON TOP OF THE SNOW COVERED BREAKWATER.

HOW SWEET... ♡
A HOME-MADE CAKE!
Merry Xm
NANA
I FEEL SO SPECIAL.
LET'S EAT! ♡
MIGHT BE POISONED...
FROM ONE OF MY FANS.
"NANA MIGHT HAVE SOMETHING GOING ON WITH REN SO DIE" CAKE.
......
THEN CHECK IT.
.....
HEY, I DON'T WANNA BE OFFED BY SOME RANDOM FREAK.
ME, NEITHER.
....

IT HAPPENED SO FAST...
I FORGOT TO CLOSE MY EYES.
THIS MAKES IT A FREAK I KNOW...
SO NOW I CAN DIE IN PEACE.
I THOUGHT I WAS GONNA DIE...
'CAUSE I WANTED REN.
I WANTED HIM SO BAD I COULDN'T DEAL...

...EVER SINCE THAT FIRST NIGHT.
DIDN'T YOU SAY, FOR THE SAKE OF THE BAND ...
NO ONE SHOULD GO OUT WITH NANA?
....
IT'S COOL MAN.
I HAVE EVERYTHING I NEED RIGHT HERE.
...ARE YOU FOR REAL?

SID &
NANCY
LOVE KILLS
WE MOVED IN TOGETHER RIGHT AWAY.
NANA
REN HONJO
NANA OSAKI
SID &
NANC
REN INSPIRED ME...
TO SING MY GUTS OUT...
TO LEARN GUITAR...
AND TO REALLY LIVE.

DOCUMENTAIRE VISUEL
TOKYO
BUT WHAT COULD I...
OFFER REN?
MAYBE IF I QUIT SING-ING...
AND MOVED TO TOKYO WITH REN...
I COULD MAKE DINNER FOR US EVERY DAY AND CLEAN THE APART-MENT.
AND HAVE HIS CHIL-DREN.
IS THAT WHAT I SHOULD BE DOING?
THAT MIGHT BE MORE THAN ENOUGH HAPPINESS.

NEITHER OF US HAD FAMILIES.

CREATING AN ALTERNATIVE FAMILY...

INSTEAD OF CHASING PIPE DREAMS...

MIGHT BE THE BEST THING FOR US.

YEP.
GUITAR AND CIGARETTES, THAT'S ALL I NEED.
LIKE ADAM* FROM "THE EVIL EYE."
YEAH, RIGHT.
HE'S SENDING IT ALL THROUGH A DELIVERY SERVICE.
SOMETHING ABOUT NOT LIKING "HEAVY STUFF."
YEAH, 'CAUSE NOW YOU WON'T HAVE ME TO BOSS AROUND AND CARRY YOUR STUFF.
I CAN SEE THE HARDSHIP ALREADY.
* Adam is a character from a previous Ai Yazawa manga.
WELL, I GUESS IT'S TIME.

GUGH!

CLAANNGG

IT'D BEEN ONE YEAR AND THREE MONTHS SINCE I MOVED IN WITH REN...
RIGHT AROUND THE BEGIN-NING OF SPRING, WHEN THERE WAS STILL SNOW ON THE GROUND.

IT
WAS
OVER.

WE DIDN'T SAY IT.
BUT WE BOTH KNEW THAT LIVING APART...
WOULD BE THE END OF US.
THERE WAS NO REASON TO CALL OR WRITE.
THERE'S NO MEANING WITHOUT TOUCH.
THE LONELINESS THAT REN COULDN'T EXPRESS...
MANIFESTED ITSELF IN BED EVERY NIGHT.
I COULD FEEL IT.

I
FELT IT
MORE
THAN
ANYONE
ELSE
COULD.

MERRY CHRIST-MAS!
WE'RE BLAST!
I MISS THAT TIME.
居酒屋
SINCE REN LEFT ...
MY DAYS ARE SPENT IN A WALKING DREAM.

ESPE-
CIALLY
ON A
SNOWY
NIGHT
LIKE
THIS.

TRAPNEST
NEW SINGLE
WINTER GARDEN

ON A COLD NIGHT LIKE THIS...
SOME-ONE, PLEASE WARM THAT MAN.
SID & NANCY
LOVE KILLS
NANA--
I GOT YOUR SELF-RELEASED CD! IT'S SO RAD!! NANA, YOUR SONGS CHEER ME UP AND INSPIRE ME. YOUR LYRICS REALLY SPEAK TO ME AS A GIRL. I WISH MORE PEOPLE COULD HEAR YOUR SONGS. BUT I MIGHT BE LONELY WHEN YOU GET FAMOUS. REN IS A ROCK STAR AND ALL THAT NOW... I'M HAPPY FOR HIM, BUT IT'S ALSO KINDA WEIRD... BUT IT'S COOL MAN, I'LL FORGIVE HIM (HEH HEH)! DO YOU GUYS KEEP IN TOUCH, NANA? PLEASE GIVE HIM MY BEST! AND MY BEST TO YOU TOO, NANA! I'LL ALWAYS, ALWAYS CHEER YOU ON.
AKIKO
P.S. LOVE THE NEW 'DO! MAYBE I'LL COPY YOU!
NANA
From Misato
Merry X'mas NANA

Merry Xmas NANA
......
SWEET ...
IT'S BEEN ONE YEAR AND NINE MONTHS SINCE REN LEFT...
ALMOST TWO SPRINGS AGO.

FOR MY 20TH BIRTH-DAY IN MARCH ...

I'M GOING TO REWARD MYSELF FOR HANGING IN THERE ...

... WITH A ONE-WAY TICKET TO TOKYO.

PACK THOSE BAGS ...
GUITAR AND CIGAR-ETTES, THAT'S ALL I NEED.

WHERE WAS I BORN?

WHAT ARE YA GONNA DO--
ASK ME?

—ジュンコ—

*Chapters of *Nana* are originally published in a Japanese magazine called *Cookie*. -ED

REALLY? COOL!
THANK YOU, DEMON LORD. ♡
BUT THERE MIGHT BE DIFFERENT NANAS CONTINUOUSLY BEING INTRODUCED WITHIN THE SERIALIZED STORYLINE, RIGHT?
HEY, THIS COULD GET INTER-ESTING.
PROB-ABLY NOT...
'CAUSE THE STORY THIS TIME WAS A PROLOGUE.
OH!
BUT WAIT!
THERE'S ALREADY TWO NANAS ...
WHAT IF THAT'S THE "NANA" THAT GETS SERIAL-IZED?!
NANA
by Nana
SNICKER
IT COULD HAPPEN.
THAT NANA'S A MUCH STRONGER CHARAC-TER.
YOU'RE RIGHT, IT PROB-ABLY WILL ...
'CAUSE I'M CURSED...
I DIDN'T MAKE THE COVER OF THIS MANGA, EITHER.
I LOSE OUT TO THE COOL GIRL ONCE AGAIN ...
THIS COULD GET UGLY...
....
WELL, IT'S FUN TO READ.
Cookie
WILL THE BONUS PAGE HAVE POST-CARDS FROM THE READERS LIKE IN "GOKINJYO" ("NEIGHBOR-HOOD") ?
"NEIGHBOR-HOOD"?
WHAT THE HELL'S THAT?
WHAT TO DO ...
I GUESS I'LL HAVE TO DO THE "PLEASE GIMME A BREAK" CORNER, BUT I DON'T WANNA.
"COOKIE" COMES OUT EVERY MONTH. SO Y'ALL GO BUY IT!
IF IT SUCKS, IT FLOPS.
"GIMME A BREAK" ?
A BUNCH OF CHAR-ACTER SKETCHES HAVE ALREADY COME IN.
REALLY?
LEMME SEE, LEMME SEE!

GRAND OPENING, NEXT ISSUE!! (PROBABLY!)

The creator, Ai Yazawa, told us, "I created this story so that it could be enjoyed as a stand-alone and, at the same time, have a complete ending that could be connected to an ongoing series. I hope you'll look forward to the future of the two Nanas!"

Ai Yazawa is the creator of many popular manga titles, including *Tenshi Nanka Janai* (I'm No Angel) and *Gokinjo Monogatari* (Neighborhood Story). Another series, *Kagen no Tsuki* (Last Quarter), was made into a live-action movie and released in late 2004. American readers were introduced to Yazawa's stylish and sexy storytelling in 2002 when her title *Paradise Kiss* was translated into English.

Nana has become the all-time best-selling shojo title from Japanese publishing giant, Shueisha. Cumulative sales from the first 12 graphic novels have sold more than 22 million copies, and the series even garnered a Shogakukan Manga Award in the girls category in 2003. A live-action *Nana* movie is scheduled to hit Japanese theaters in the fall of 2005.

NANA
VOL. 1

Shojo Beat Edition

This manga volume contains material that was originally published in English in *Shojo Beat* magazine, #1–2.

STORY AND ART BY AI YAZAWA

English Adaptation/Allison Wolfe
Translation/Koji Goto
Touch-up Art & Lettering/Sabrina Heep
Design/Courtney Utt
Editor/Eric Searleman

Printed in the U.S.A.

Published by VIZ Media, LLC
P.O. Box 77010
San Francisco, CA 94107

13
First printing, November 2005
Thirteenth printing, September 2021

PARENTAL ADVISORY
NANA is rated T+ for Older Teen and is recommended for ages 16 and up. This volume contains strong language and sexual situations.
ratings.viz.com

www.viz.com www.shojobeat.com

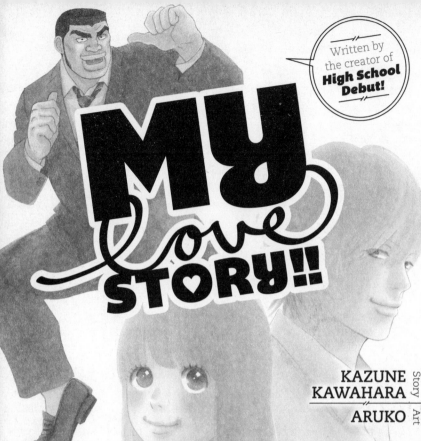

Lydia can see fairies—

but can she tell who the real villain is?

The Earl & the Fairy

Story & Art by Ayuko

Original Concept by Mizue Tani

Lydia Carlton is a fairy doctor, one of the few people with the ability to see the magical creatures who share our world. During one of her rare trips to London to visit her father, Lydia's quiet life is suddenly transformed when she is rescued from kidnappers by a mysterious young man!

Check your local manga retailer for availability!

Vol. 1 ~ ISBN: 978-1-4215-4168-6
Vol. 2 ~ ISBN: 978-1-4215-4169-3
Vol. 3 ~ ISBN: 978-1-4215-4170-9
Vol. 4 ~ ISBN: 978-1-4215-4171-6

VIZ Shojo Beat RATED T TEEN

Demon Love Spell

STORY AND ART BY
MAYU SHINJO

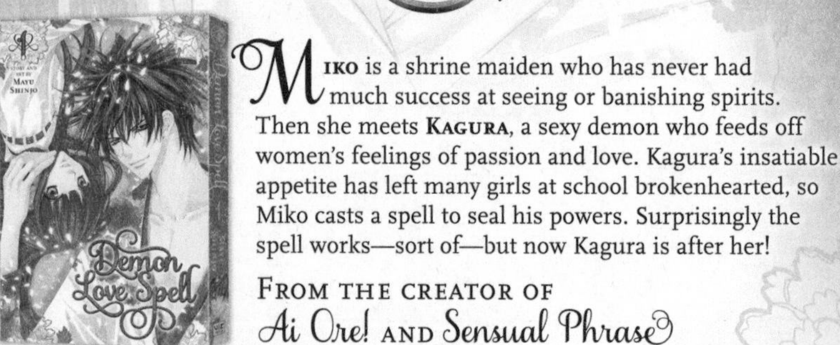

Shojo Beat

ON SALE NOW!

Honey So Sweet

Story and Art by Amu Meguro

Little did Nao Kogure realize back in middle school that when she left an umbrella and a box of bandages in the rain for injured delinquent Taiga Onise that she would meet him again in high school. Nao wants nothing to do with the gruff and frightening Taiga, but he suddenly presents her with a huge bouquet of flowers and asks her to date him—with marriage in mind! Is Taiga really so scary, or is he a sweetheart in disguise?

SURPRISE!

You may be reading the wrong way!

It's true: In keeping with the original Japanese comic format, this book reads from right to left—so action, sound effects, and word balloons are completely reversed. This preserves the orientation of the original artwork—plus, it's fun! Check out the diagram shown here to get the hang of things, and then turn to the other side of the book to get started!

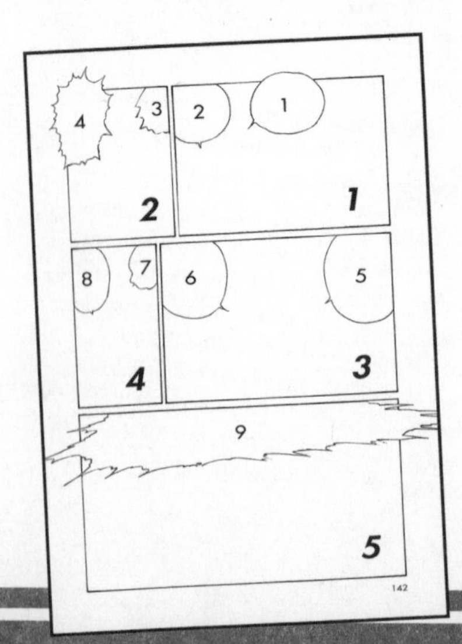